W9-CPM-617

TIMBER PRESS
POCKET GUIDE TO
*Palms*

TIMBER PRESS
POCKET GUIDE TO
# *Palms*

ROBERT LEE RIFFLE

TIMBER PRESS

Frontispiece: *Cocos nucifera,* the coconut palm tree, is without doubt the universally recognized emblem of the tropics.

Published in 2008 by
Timber Press, Inc.
The Haseltine Building
133 S.W. Second Avenue, Suite 450
Portland, Oregon 97204-3527, U.S.A.

www.timberpress.com

For contact information regarding editorial, marketing, sales, and distribution in the United Kingdom, see www.timberpress.co.uk

Designed by Christi Payne
Printed through Colorcraft Ltd., Hong Kong

Library of Congress Cataloging-in-Publication Data

Riffle, Robert Lee.
    Timber Press pocket guide to palms / Robert Lee Riffle.
        p. cm.
    Includes bibliographical references and index.
    ISBN-13: 978-0-88192-776-4
 1.   Palms. I. Title. II. Title: Pocket guide to palms. II. Title: Palms.

    SB413.P17R54 2008
    635.9'345—dc22
                                                2007002626

A catalog record for this book is also available from the British Library.

*All photographs are by the author unless otherwise noted.*

## Acknowledgments

My thanks to all the individuals and institutions mentioned in *An Encyclopedia of Cultivated Palms*, on which this pocket guide is based. Special thanks to Paul Craft, my encyclopedia co-author, for supporting the preparation of this guide and providing new photographs. I also want to thank the other individuals who contributed photographs for this edition: Martin Gibbons, Chuck Hubbuch, Rolf Kyburz, Nancy Landau, Bryan Laughland, Bo-Göran Lundkvist, Barry Osborne, Tobias Spanner, Forrest and Kim Starr, Gaston Torres-Vera, and Richard Travis.

## About This Book

The entries in this pocket guide are arranged in alphabetical order by scientific name. If a genus or species name appears to be missing from this alphabetical listing, it may be because the name has been changed by taxonomists. To find the current name, look up the "missing" name in the index, which provides a page reference to the correct name. Common names and synonyms are given where appropriate. Each plant description is followed by cultivation notes and includes hardiness zone numbers based on the United States Department of Agriculture map.

## Publisher's Note

The publisher would like to thank the following individuals for their help in readying this manuscript for publication: Paul Craft, Don Hodel, Diane Laird, Larry Noblick, and Scott Zona.

# CONTENTS

Opposite: Young trunks of *Acrocomia aculeata*, the macaw palm, are covered with vicious spines that may drop off as the tree matures but meanwhile pose a threat to any passersby. Paul Craft

# PREFACE

This book is intended for gardeners of all levels of experience. It includes concise descriptions of the palms likely to be found in cultivation. A few species that are uncommon but definitely deserving of wider cultivation are also mentioned for the adventurous gardeners wishing to experiment.

The plants illustrated and described in this pocket guide are primarily species. Sports, cultivars (with few exceptions), and mutations have been omitted to keep the focus on knowing, growing, and preserving what nature has given us.

Many of the species come from subtropical and tropical climates as expected, but even so are suitable to temperate climates. Palms in the latter group may freeze to the ground in winter, but as long as the growing point remains protected underground, the plant will resprout in spring when warmer weather appears.

Vital to this text is the cultivation information. Each description indicates the plant's preferred growing conditions, whether wet and humid, dry and Mediterranean, or something in between. Other details necessary for successful cultivation indoors and outdoors are presented, such as hardiness zone(s), water and light requirements, type of soil, and salt and wind tolerances. Distribution data offer still additional clues on where and how to best grow the palms. And finally, for those who wish to grow their own plants, the text provides notes on germinating seed.

Because palms are often underutilized or improperly sited, even surprisingly in the tropics and subtropics, this book gives suggested landscape uses. Some are general guidelines; others depend on the specific ornamental characteristics of a given palm, such as habit, trunk, crownshaft, leaves, flowers, and fruit.

Where possible, key plant features have been illustrated. The photographs show plants in cultivation as well as in their habitats. In both instances the country or state is indicated for the plants shown.

Opposite: The persistent shag, or "skirt," of dead leaves on all but old plants of *Copernicia macroglossa*, Cuban petticoat palm, adds drama to the landscape.

# INTRODUCTION

What is a palm? A palm is first of all a flowering plant. This distinguishes it from nonflowering plants such as conifers. Although palms are usually grown for their architectural form or economic value (for example, oil, food, or fiber), they can produce outstanding flower clusters. *Corypha umbraculifera*, the talipot palm from India, bears the world's largest flower clusters, reaching 20–30 ft. (6–9 m) tall by 30–40 ft. (9–12 m) wide, while its close relative *C. utan* bears small but numerous flowers, by some counts up to 15 million on a single plant.

Second, a palm is a monocot, meaning that it has one embryo or seed leaf, mostly nonwoody tissues, and flower parts in threes or multiples of three. This distinguishes it from the dicots, a group of flowering plants with two seed leaves, mostly woody tissues, and flowering parts in fives or multiples of five. Palms are among the few monocot families with woody tissues. Other monocot families are bananas, aroids (for example, philodendrons and calla lilies), orchids, bromeliads, heliconias, cannas, and all grasses including corn.

What is not a palm? The answer is cycads, aloes, yuccas, and similar-looking large and usually woody plants, all of which outwardly resemble palms. Cycads especially look like palms but are not even flowering plants; rather they are more closely related to conifers.

## Palm Structure

Palm species may be shrublike, treelike, or vinelike. Only a few palms naturally produce branch-

*Roystonea regia* stand at Montgomery Botanical Center in Miami, Florida. Paul Craft

Opposite: Clothed with leaves from top to bottom, *Acoelorraphe wrightii*, the Everglades palm, is eminently suitable for use in the landscape as an isolated specimen or in a hedge or screen.

ing trunks, but many abnormally produce subsidiary stems from points above the ground, the abnormality usually caused by an injury to the stem. Leaves of all types are produced only from the ends of the stems or trunks. The only growth form not represented in the family is that of the true epiphyte.

Palm species include those with a solitary trunk and those with clustering or clumping stems. Dimensions range from an ultimate height of 6 in. (15 cm) to at least 150 ft. (45 m) and a stem diameter of ⅛ in. (3 mm) to 6 ft. (1.8 m). Palm trunks are graced with the scars of former leaves in the crown; these scars may be prominent and are generally semicircular. Otherwise the stems may be more or less smooth or variously adorned with the remains of old and dead leaves, including spines or other protrusions. Palm stems may grow straight as an arrow, leaning to one side (usually necessarily the case in densely clumping species), or horizontally above the ground or even below it.

As monocots, palms do not increase their trunk size by growing new wood. Rather, if the trunk enlarges, it does so by expanding the tissues first formed. This characteristic has one important implication for gardeners: injuries to palm trunks are permanent and cannot be repaired by the plants. Also, since few of the trunked palms branch naturally, killing or removing the growing point means the death of that stem and, in the case of solitary-trunked species, the death of the plant.

Similar to other tropical rain forest plants, some palms develop aboveground stilt roots to support the main trunk. These structures are usually associated with species which begin their lives as undergrowth subjects and grow quickly upwards to attain the sunlight they need to mature. Most palms have relatively shallow root systems. This fact is important to remember when growing palms: they are mainly surface feeders and need regular applications of moisture.

A palm leaf consists of a sheath, a petiole, and a blade. The sheath is a broadened tubular part, at least until the leaf has emerged entirely from the growing point. After the leaf emerges, the sheath may remain large and tubular or it may split as does the blade of the expanding leaf. Beyond the sheath is the petiole, or leaf stalk, which ranges from long to so short as to not be apparent. And beyond the petiole is the blade, the most obvious part of the leaf. The blade may be entire (unsegmented), feather-shaped (pinnate), or fan-shaped (palmate).

The segments of pinnate leaves may be completely free of each other, fused, or partly fused; they may also be further segmented or entire. The individual segments of pinnate leaves are referred to as the leaflets. The leaflets may grow in one plane from the leaf stalk to create a flat or nearly flat leaf in cross-section, or they may grow from the leaf stalk at an angle that creates a V-shaped leaf in cross-section. In palmate leaves the blade may be entire or divided into segments of various widths and lengths; these segments may be further segmented or not.

The size of palm leaves, including sheath, petiole, and blade, ranges from less than a foot (30 cm) long to more than 70 ft. (21 m) long, the largest leaf among the flowering plants. Only giant kelps in the Pacific Ocean have longer leaves and they are not flowering plants. Like palm stems, palm leaves may bear spines or other protrusions.

The palmate leaf of *Coccothrinax miraguama*, in Cuba. Paul Craft

The pinnate leaf of *Chamaedorea microspadix*, the hardy bamboo palm, in Texas.

Sprays of white flowers on pinkish red branches of *Pinanga coronata*, the ivory cane palm, in Florida. Paul Craft

The sheaths of palm leaves may form a crownshaft at the top of the trunk. The crownshaft is a cylindrical, columnar organ that may be tiny or grand, green or beautifully colored, and may bear hairs, threads, or spines to match the rest of the leaf.

Compared to the flowers of most other plant families, palm flowers are small. Many are significantly under an inch (2.5 cm) in diameter; however, they are invariably formed in large clusters called *inflorescences*. The inflorescences may grow from the leaf crown in the same manner as the leaves, or they may grow below the leaves at nodes on the trunks or even directly from the top of the stem. The latter phenomenon results in the slow death of the stem from which the inflorescence grows.

Palm fruits range from small to gigantic and, like the inflorescences, are borne in large or small clusters. They may be smooth or covered in scales or spines, and their surfaces may be soft or hard and woody. They normally contain only one seed in the center of the flesh, but the flesh may be almost nonexistent and there may be as many as 10 seeds in one fruit. Some fruits are edible, such as the coconut and date palms.

## Palm Habitats

Palms are indigenous to every continent except Antarctica. The northernmost naturally occurring genus (*Chamaerops*) is distributed in Europe, and the southernmost naturally occurring genus (*Rhopalostylis*) is found in New Zealand.

Palm habitats include all types except cold montane regions and polar regions. Species are found in mangrove coastal environments, estuaries, and fresh water swamps, desert oases, tropical and subtropical coastal plains and grasslands, deciduous tropical forests, rain forests (both lowland and montane and both tropical and warm temperate), and even in the drier regions of mountains. At least one species is a true aquatic. The greatest diversity of palms occurs in tropical forest regions, especially humid and moist forests where many smaller palm species are undergrowth subjects, the larger species at home in clearings and along riverbanks.

14

## Palms in the Landscape

Palms are the most underused design elements in nearly every garden, even most of those in the tropics or subtropics. Fortunate indeed are gardeners who live in regions where at least a few palms grow, as their unique variety of forms cannot begin to be simulated by anything other than massive ferns, yuccas, and cordylines, which themselves are tropical or subtropical.

The biggest reason these princes of the plant world are eschewed even where they can be grown is probably lack of space: most palm species are relatively large. This problem is compounded by the gardener's desire for color. The desire is, of course, an important one, but color is greatly overused at the expense of variety of

The colorful stems of *Cyrtostachys renda*, the sealing-wax palm, in Florida.

form. The smaller the garden, the more the use of color alone tends to become overwhelming and even tiring, somewhat analogous to eating a diet of cake and ice cream only, or listening to only one type of music. *Variety* is the operative word and is what palms excel at with their wonderfully different forms. In addition, palms are often colorful, especially the tropical species. Their crownshafts, inflorescences, and leaf colors are sometimes extraordinary. Palms lend to the landscape a more controlled and subtle color palette than that of most other strictly "flowering plants."

A few points should be considered when incorporating palms into the landscape. First, palms usually do not look good planted in straight lines. But what type of plant does? This arrangement is unnatural in the sense that it does not occur in nature. The larger palms are magnificence itself when lining paths or streets, but the dictum still applies: a curving street, path, or driveway is infinitely more aesthetically pleasing than a straight one where variety is the missing element.

Second, palms generally look their best when planted in small groups or groves rather than as a single tree surrounded by space. Again, the reason is that palms very seldom occur singly in nature. Furthermore the discrete groups look best when the number of individuals therein is three or more and the individuals are of varying heights; if each palm is the same height, the crowns visually "fight." Variety is the missing element in groups of same-height palms.

Third, a landscape whose horizon is at one level is incredibly less interesting and beautiful than one of varying levels. Nothing fixes the imbalance better than using palms as canopyscapes, where the crowns of trees float above the general level of the surrounding vegetation. Such palms substitute remarkably well for a lack of mountains. Again, variety of form.

Fourth, the wall of vegetation that constitutes the horizon of the garden is so much less appealing if it is of one form or of one color. No plants are better suited to fix this condition than palms, whether large or small, fan-leaved (palmate) or feather-leaved (pinnate). Palms are the *sine-qua-non* elements that create the needed form and texture. Again, variety of form.

A few palm species are so large and impressive that they can be advantageously planted alone as specimens or accents surrounded by space and still look good. They would look even better if planted in groups, but the size or other limitations of a given landscape or garden can often make this difficult or impossible.

Finally, no palm species has an uninteresting or ugly silhouette, so palms can be planted in front of walls or other structures, especially if the structure has a contrasting color. In this situation even small palms can look wonderful planted singly.

## Pruning

Once planted in the landscape, palms tend to be lamentably overpruned. The reason for this is partly that they are unlike other garden trees and shrubs with which most gardeners are more familiar. Most people agonize all too much about whether to prune a palm tree, thinking, naturally enough, that a palm is like a hydrangea bush, an oak tree, or a morning-glory vine that needs diligent guidance from youth to old age to make a presentable landscape specimen. This is not the case. A palm occasionally requires some pruning, but the type and frequency of pruning requirements are unlike those of other landscape subjects. A palm is, except for some special aesthetic concerns, human safety, or the health of the plant itself, a low-maintenance landscape subject.

### Aesthetic Concerns

Several palm species, like *Washingtonia filifera* and *W. robusta*, have a characteristic and mostly picturesque shag, sometimes called a *petticoat* or *skirt*. These petticoats consist of the adherent dead leaves whose leaf bases often refuse to fall from the trunk. In the palms' native desert and arid grassland regions, natural fires commonly burn off the old leaves. In cultivation, the palms seldom retain enough dead leaves in moist and humid climes to form the petticoat but, in more arid regions, they usually do. Some palm own-

ers love the shag, while others detest the "ugly haystack." The easiest way to remove the shag is, of course, one leaf at a time, as the individual leaves die and become pendent.

Then there is the manicurist mentality of those who want palms like *Washingtonia robusta* to have clean and smooth trunks from the bottom all the way to the leaf crown. This look is popular, especially in fantasy parks and Las Vegas. Removing all adherent leaf bases from these palms creates an undeniably handsome look because of the elegantly thin and smooth, tall trunks, but the procedure is both time consuming and labor intensive, especially for tall specimens.

The fiber-covered stem of *Coccothrinax crinita*, the old man palm, in Florida.

The immense, rounded canopy of *Phoenix canariensis*, the Canary Island date palm, in Florida.

*Washingtonia robusta*, for example, can grow rather quickly to a height of 40 ft. (12 m), and old palms may attain a height of 100 ft. (30 m).

The leaf bases of some palms fall off at various times, but in other palms the blades fall off while the leaf bases themselves, and sometimes most of the leaf stalk, adhere to the trunk for some time. A prime example of the latter is *Sabal palmetto* in the southeastern United States. The dead leaf bases may adhere for most of the life of this slow-growing palm, turning woody and much lighter colored than the actual trunk, and giving a picturesque wicker look to the trunk. Often these woody leaf bases are trimmed with a chain saw to conform one to the other in appearance and to create an even more elegant and manicured look.

Some popular palms like *Phoenix canariensis* (Canary Island date palm) produce immense, rounded canopies of long pinnate leaves. I personally consider this aspect of the species its most desirable trait, but others feel the palm looks better when the pendent leaves are removed, allowing only the leaves that do not fall below the horizontal plane to remain on the trunk. Removing the pendent leaves is no more difficult than removing the petticoats of *Washingtonia* palms and, since *P. canariensis* grows more slowly than either *Washingtonia* species, the task need not be done as often.

Most pruners leave the leaf bases of the just-cut crop of leaves, which practice results in a picturesque, large rounded knobby cluster (called the *bulb* or *pineapple*) of leaf bases directly beneath the leaf crown. By the time of the next leaf pruning, the bulb of leaf bases will have mostly fallen away from the trunk naturally. Other pruners remove the bulb also, which results in an even more picturesque tree with a more tropical and more airy aspect.

Unfortunately, many palm owners or the landscapers they hire go far beyond these pruning practices: they remove enough leaves to create leaf crowns that look like feather dusters or shuttlecocks, leaving only the most erect, living leaves. This abominable practice completely ruins the wonderful appearance of these species. It is

also inimical to the overall health of the tree which must struggle to photosynthesize enough food to maintain itself. Alas, this misguided practice is not limited to *Phoenix* species. It is all too common to see *Washingtonia*, *Syagrus romanzoffiana*, and many other species cropped in this manner, especially by plant maintenance contractors who, of course, make more money by recommending the monthly butchering of these beauties.

Several clustering palm species have unique aesthetic and maintenance characteristics. A prime example is *Phoenix reclinata*, which forms many suckers (subsidiary trunks) throughout its life; a single specimen may have up to two dozen trunks. The trunks are not straight but lean gracefully outward from their points of origin. Few natural phenomena are as beautiful as a large "tuft" of this palm, but the clumps are made even more graceful and dramatic if a few trunks are thinned out as the mass develops,

The distinct spiral pattern of persistent leaf bases on *Corypha utan*, in Australia. Paul Craft

leaving trunks of differing heights. This allows the individual beauty of each trunk and the exquisitely graceful tableau of trunks and crowns to be seen and appreciated to its fullest. The trunks should be thinned when they are young and short, using a large pair of lopping shears to cut off the growing point; when the trunk decays sufficiently, it can easily be pulled apart.

## Human Safety

For most palms the rapidity with which the dead leaf parts fall from the trunks is a matter of environmental conditions, such as wind, abrasion, fire, rain, and humidity. Then there is vandalism. In some locations, juvenile (and sometimes not so juvenile) miscreants create "fireworks" by setting ablaze the shags of *Washingtonia* and other petticoat-forming species. Such conflagrations may also be induced by the careless tossing of live cigarettes and cigars from passersby as well as lightning strikes and even (in rare instances) damaged live electrical wires. Furthermore, masses of dead and dry leaves can be a habitat of vermin, obnoxious bird species, scorpions, rats, mice, and even small snakes. (Of course, palm "skirts" are just as likely to harbor "good" birds, as well as endangered and beneficial animals such as bats and vermin-eating snakes.)

It is better to refrain from planting a tree where it can become undesirable, looking crowded and cramped, or where it can obstruct a desirable view. In practice, however, such problems often arise because the person who planted the palm did not know the ultimate dimensions of the particular species or just wanted its juvenile look for a certain period. In many instances the desirable, ultimate, and overall landscape use of the palm warrants temporary pruning of its leaves, so that in time it becomes a positive component of the landscape. In such instances at least half of the leaves must be allowed to remain for the health and continued functioning of the tree. If too many leaves are removed, over time a trunk that should be columnar or naturally tapering will exhibit unsightly bulges and constrictions, reflecting the varying amounts of sugar it could produce at a given point.

Few palms produce large enough leaves or grow tall enough for their falling leaves to be much of a danger, but some, like the coconut (*Cocos nucifera*), large date palms (for example, *Phoenix canariensis*), and royals (*Roystonea* species), attain great heights and have large, heavy leaves with massive leaf stalks and midribs. In addition, the coconut produces clusters of large, heavy fruit whose natural separation from the stalk and consequent rapid descent when ripe can (in rare instances) be deadly. Removing the leaves and fruits from tall specimens is labor intensive, especially if there are many trees requiring such pruning.

A few tropical palm species have natural rings of large spines at regular intervals around their trunks. Among these are the macaw and grugru palms, *Acrocomia* species. Such spines are easily removed with shears or small branch cutters. Much more common are palm species with vicious spines on part of the leaves. Prime examples are all *Phoenix* species (date palms) whose lower (basal) leaflets are always metamorphosed into spines of varying lengths and viciousness. When young, the older, lower, and more spreading leaves of these palms are often removed if they are near human pathways.

## Health of the Palm

Only two situations call for pruning a palm to maintain its health: at transplanting and to cure or prevent disease. Leaf pruning, especially of bare-root or balled-and-burlapped plants, is usually a necessity when transplanting. Removing at least half the leaf crown is usually recommended in these cases to reduce moisture loss through transpiration because of the inevitable root loss. Indeed, with all *Sabal* species the recommendation is to remove all leaves except the spear, or newest unfurled leaf, as the roots of this palm supposedly die under such circumstances and the palm will have to grow an entirely new set from the trunk.

Several types of fungus infestations are cured or prevented by leaf removal. The two most common fungal problems are *Graphiola* leaf smut (false smut) and diamond scale. The latter,

Immature fruit of *Cocos nucifera* 'Golden Malayan Dwarf', a form of the coconut palm, at The Kampong in Coral Gables, Florida.

in spite of the name, is not a scale insect but rather a fungus which produces scalelike lesions. The fungus must first be identified and then the leaves with the worst infestations should be completely removed and burned before finally applying the proper fungicide to the tree. In California, a deadly and incurable fungal disease (*Fusarium* wilt) is transferred by pruning tools, as the fungus organism resides in the sap of the tree. In all cases, but especially in California, pruning tools should be sterilized between pruning one palm tree and another.

*Dypsis decipiens* is imposing in the landscape, in California. Barry Osborne

# CULTIVATED PALMS
# FOR SPECIFIC PURPOSES AND LOCATIONS

## Drought-Tolerant Palms

No palm is truly drought tolerant in the sense that most cactus species are, and even palms growing in the Sahara do so at or near springs or other underground water sources. Furthermore, most palm species occur in tropical rain forest. Despite these disclaimers, a number of species thrive without copious moisture, can survive extended periods of deprivation, and can withstand drying winds.

*Acrocomia* (some)
*Allagoptera arenaria* (great)
*Arenga pinnata* (some)
*Bismarckia nobilis* (much)
*Borassus* (much)
*Brahea armata* (much)
*Brahea decumbens* (much)
*Butia capitata* (some)
*Chamaerops humilis* (much)
*Coccothrinax* (much)
*Cocos nucifera* (much when established)
*Copernicia alba* (some)
*Copernicia baileyana* (some)
*Copernicia hospita* (some)
*Copernicia macroglossa* (some)
*Copernicia prunifera* (some)
*Corypha umbraculifera* (some when established)
*Dypsis decaryi* (much)
*Dypsis decipiens* (much)
*Guihaia argyrata* (some)
*Hyphaene* (much)
*Jubaea chilensis* (much when established)
*Latania* (some)
*Livistona chinensis* (some)
*Livistona drudei* (some)
*Livistona mariae* (much when established)
*Livistona nitida* (some)
*Nannorrhops ritchiana* (very much)
*Phoenix canariensis* (much when established)
*Phoenix dactylifera* (much when established)
*Phoenix reclinata* (some)
*Phoenix sylvestris* (much when established)
*Pseudophoenix sargentii* (much)
*Rhapis* (some)
*Sabal causiarum* (some)
*Sabal domingensis* (some)
*Sabal mauritiiformis* (some when established)
*Sabal mexicana* (much when established)
*Sabal palmetto* (some)
*Sabal uresana* (much)
*Serenoa repens* (much)
*Syagrus coronata* (much)
*Syagrus schizophylla* (much)
*Thrinax excelsa* (some)
*Thrinax morrisii* (much)
*Thrinax radiata* (much)
*Trithrinax* (much)
*Washingtonia filifera* (much when established)
*Washingtonia robusta* (some when established)
*Zombia antillarum* (some)

## Water-Loving Palms

Most palm species benefit from regular amounts of water, but several have extraordinary water requirements even when established. Some are considered aquatics.

*Acoelorraphe wrightii*
*Areca triandra*
*Carpentaria acuminata*
*Chamaedorea cataractarum*
*Cyrtostachys renda*
*Elaeis guineensis*
*Euterpe oleracea*
*Euterpe precatoria*
*Hydriastele costata*
*Livistona australis*
*Metroxylon sagu*
*Nypa fruticans*
*Oncosperma tigillarium*

*Phoenix roebelinii*
*Ptychosperma macarthurii*
*Raphia*
*Ravenea rivularis*
*Rhapidophyllum hystrix*
*Roystonea regia*
*Sabal minor*

## Fast-Growing Palms

Very few palm species are considered fast grow-ing when compared to other tree families, and some are exceedingly slow. The following list includes palms that are faster than the average, assuming the plants are given optimum growing conditions.

*Acrocomia* (moderately)
*Adonidia merrillii* (moderately)
*Aiphanes aculeata* (moderately)
*Archontophoenix alexandrae* (moderately)
*Archontophoenix cunninghamiana*
   (moderately)
*Areca catechu* (quite)
*Areca triandra* (moderately)
*Arenga pinnata* (moderately)
*Astrocaryum mexicanum* (moderately)
*Bactris gasipaes* (moderately)
*Carpentaria acuminata* (quite)
*Caryota* (quite)
*Chambeyronia macrocarpa* (moderately)
*Cocos nucifera* (moderately)
*Dypsis lutescens* (moderately)
*Euterpe edulis* (moderately)
*Euterpe oleracea* (moderately)
*Heterospathe elata* (moderately)
*Licuala peltata* (moderately)
*Licuala spinosa* (moderately)
*Livistona chinensis* (moderately)
*Livistona decora* (moderately to quite)
*Livistona mariae* (moderately)
*Livistona nitida* (moderately)
*Metroxylon* (quite)
*Nypa fruticans* (moderately)
*Oncosperma tigillarium* (moderately)
*Phoenix reclinata* (moderately)
*Phoenix rupicola* (moderately)
*Ravenea rivularis* (moderately)

*Roystonea oleracea* (moderately)
*Roystonea regia* (moderately)
*Syagrus romanzoffiana* (very)
*Veitchia* (quite)
*Washingtonia filifera* (moderately)
*Washingtonia robusta* (quite)

## Very Slow Growing Palms

Although all palms are relatively slow growing compared to other tree families, some are ex-tremely slow growing.

*Attalea*
*Coccothrinax*
*Copernicia*
*Guihaia argyrata*
*Hedyscepe canterburyana*
*Howea belmoreana*
*Hyphaene*
*Johannesteijsmannia*
*Jubaea chilensis*
*Jubaeopsis caffra*
*Licuala*
*Lytocaryum weddellianum*
*Parajubaea*
*Pritchardia hillebrandii*
*Pseudophoenix sargentii*
*Rhapidophyllum hystrix*
*Sabal*
*Zombia antillarum*

## Groundcovering Palms

Short palms that creep by aboveground or un-derground stems can be used in the landscape as groundcovers. Others are amenable for mass plantings because of their size and form.

*Arenga caudata*
*Brahea decumbens*
*Chamaedorea cataractarum*
*Chamaedorea elegans*
*Chamaedorea metallica*
*Chamaedorea radicalis*
*Guihaia argyrata*
*Reinhardtia gracilis*
*Sabal minor*

## Hedge and Screen Palms

Whether practical or aesthetic in their basic function, or sometimes both, hedges and screens require palms that hold their leaves from top to bottom.

*Acoelorraphe wrightii*
*Allagoptera arenaria*
*Areca triandra*
*Arenga caudata*
*Arenga engleri*
*Arenga tremula*
*Bactris gasipaes*
*Bactris major*
*Caryota mitis*
*Chamaedorea cataractarum*
*Chamaedorea costaricana*
*Chamaedorea microspadix*
*Chamaedorea seifrizii*
*Chamaerops humilis*
*Cyrtostachys renda*
*Dypsis cabadae*
*Dypsis lutescens*
*Euterpe oleracea*
*Licuala spinosa*
*Metroxylon sagu*
*Nannorrhops ritchiana*
*Nypa fruticans*
*Oncosperma tigillarium*
*Phoenix reclinata*
*Pinanga coronata*
*Pinanga dicksonii*
*Ptychosperma macarthurii*
*Reinhardtia latisecta*
*Rhapidophyllum hystrix*
*Rhapis excelsa*
*Rhapis humilis*
*Trithrinax campestris*
*Zombia antillarum*

## Large Palms

These very tall palms normally attain a total height of 60 ft. (18 m) or more, or are otherwise massive in their proportions.

*Attalea* (most)
*Beccariophoenix madagascariensis*
*Bismarckia nobilis*

*Borassus*
*Caryota gigas*
*Caryota urens*
*Cocos nucifera*
*Copernicia alba*
*Copernicia baileyana*
*Corypha*
*Elaeis guineensis*
*Hydriastele costata*
*Hyphaene*
*Jubaea chilensis*
*Kentiopsis oliviformis*
*Livistona australis*
*Livistona drudei*
*Livistona mariae*
*Livistona nitida*
*Livistona rotundifolia*
*Livistona saribus*
*Metroxylon*
*Oncosperma tigillarium*
*Phoenix canariensis*
*Phoenix dactylifera*
*Phoenix reclinata*
*Phoenix sylvestris*
*Raphia*
*Ravenea rivularis*
*Roystonea* (most)
*Sabal causiarum*
*Sabal domingensis*
*Veitchia arecina*
*Veitchia joannis*
*Washingtonia filifera*
*Washingtonia robusta*

## Small Palms

These palms are generally under 10 ft. (3 m) total height and do not spread widely.

*Arenga caudata*
*Chamaedorea* (most)
*Guihaia argyrata*
*Licuala* (most)
*Phoenix roebelinii*
*Pinanga* (most)
*Reinhardtia gracilis*
*Rhapis excelsa*
*Sabal minor*
*Syagrus schizophylla*

## Palms Tolerant of Alkaline Soil

This category is a tricky one. Almost any palm can be made to survive in almost any soil type with heroic efforts of amendment, irrigation, and fertilization. For example, *Caryota* species generally need a rich, humus-laden, slightly acidic soil, and yet peninsular Florida, where the soil is slightly to quite alkaline, is full of most of these species. The species listed here thrive with moderate, not heroic, adjustments.

*Allagoptera arenaria* (extreme)
*Bismarckia nobilis*
*Borassus*
*Chamaerops humilis* (some)
*Coccothrinax*
*Cocos nucifera* (great)
*Copernicia* (great)
*Corypha*
*Cryosophila warscewiczii*
*Dictyosperma album* (some)
*Dypsis decaryi* (some)
*Guihaia argyrata*
*Hyophorbe* (some)
*Hyphaene* (some)
*Jubaea chilensis*
*Latania* (some)
*Livistona mariae*
*Livistona rotundifolia*
*Nannorrhops ritchiana* (some)
*Nypa fruticans* (some)
*Phoenix dactylifera* (great)
*Phoenix reclinata* (some)
*Phoenix theophrasti* (great)
*Pritchardia pacifica* (some)
*Pritchardia thurstonii* (some)
*Pseudophoenix sargentii* (some)
*Ptychosperma* (some)
*Raphia*
*Rhapidophyllum hystrix*
*Rhapis*
*Roystonea regia* (some)
*Sabal* (some to great)
*Schippia concolor* (some)
*Serenoa repens* (great)
*Syagrus schizophylla* (some)

*Thrinax* (some to great)
*Trachycarpus fortunei*
*Trithrinax* (some to great)
*Veitchia* (some)
*Washingtonia* (some)
*Zombia antillarum* (some)

## Salt-Tolerant Palms

Palms tolerate various degrees of salinity in the soil and air, ranging from slight to some, great, or extreme.

*Acoelorraphe wrightii* (some)
*Adonidia merrillii* (airborne only)
*Allagoptera arenaria* (extreme)
*Coccothrinax* (some to great)
*Cocos nucifera* (great)
*Copernicia macroglossa* (great)
*Hyophorbe lagenicaulis* (some)
*Hyophorbe verschaffeltii* (some)
*Hyphaene* (some to great)
*Licuala spinosa* (some)
*Livistona saribus* (some)
*Nannorrhops ritchiana* (some)
*Nypa fruticans* (some)
*Oncosperma tigillarium* (some)
*Phoenix canariensis* (airborne only)
*Phoenix dactylifera* (great)
*Phoenix theophrasti* (great)
*Pritchardia pacifica* (airborne)
*Pritchardia thurstonii* (airborne)
*Pseudophoenix sargentii* (great)
*Sabal mexicana* (some)
*Sabal palmetto* (some)
*Sabal uresana* (some)
*Serenoa repens* (great)
*Syagrus schizophylla* (some)
*Thrinax morrisii* (some)
*Thrinax radiata* (some)
*Veitchia* (airborne only)
*Washingtonia* (some)
*Zombia antillarum* (some)

## Palms with Colored New Growth

*Areca vestiaria* form
*Chambeyronia macrocarpa*
*Heterospathe elata*

*Laccospadix australasica*
*Pinanga coronata*
*Pinanga maculata*

## Palms with Permanently Colored Leaves or Crownshafts

*Allagoptera arenaria*
*Areca vestiaria*
*Arenga*
*Astrocaryum*
*Bismarckia nobilis*
*Brahea armata*
*Brahea decumbens*
*Butia capitata* (many forms)
*Coccothrinax*
*Copernicia alba*
*Copernicia hospita*
*Copernicia prunifera*
*Cryosophila warscewiczii*
*Cyrtostachys renda*
*Dypsis leptocheilos*
*Guihaia argyrata*
*Hyphaene* (most species)
*Johannesteijsmannia*
*Kerriodoxa elegans*
*Latania loddigesii*
*Pelagodoxa henryana*

*Pinanga coronata*
*Sabal uresana*
*Satakentia liukiuensis*
*Serenoa repens* (some forms)
*Thrinax morrisii*

## Palms for Indoors

*Chamaedorea elegans*
*Howea forsteriana*
*Laccospadix australasica*
*Licuala cordata*
*Licuala grandis*
*Licuala orbicularis*
*Lytocaryum weddellianum*
*Pinanga coronata*
*Rhapis excelsa*

## Palms for Temperate Climates

*Rhapidophyllum hystrix*
*Sabal minor*
*Sabal palmetto*
*Serenoa repens*
*Trachycarpus fortunei*
*Trachycarpus martianunus*
*Trithrinax brasiliensis*
*Trithrinax campestris*
*Washingtonia filifera*

# CULTIVATED PALMS A–Z

## Acanthophoenix rubra
### Barbel palm, red palm

**Distribution:** the Indian Ocean islands of Mauritius and Réunion **Growth habit:** solitary **Height & width:** 40 ft. (12 m) tall, 15 ft. (4.5 m) wide **Trunk(s):** 20–35 ft. (6–10.5 m) tall, upper parts very spiny, lower parts whitish with darker rings **Crownshaft:** 2–3 ft. (60–90 cm) tall, grayish green to reddish brown, bulging at the base **Leaves:** pinnate, 6–10 ft. (1.8–3 m) long, leaflets 2 ft. (60 cm) long, growing in a flat plane, with small spines when young (and sometimes when older), deep green above, lighter green beneath **Flower clusters:** many small pink, red, or purplish unisexual flowers of both sexes **Fruit:** round, ½ in. (12 mm) wide, black when ripe **Growth rate:** medium except in warmest Mediterranean climes where it grows slowly **Climate:** 10b and 11 **Exposure:** part shade when young, full sun when older **Soil:** any but benefits from organic material **Water needs:** high; grows poorly and very slowly in dry conditions **Salt tolerance:** slight; air only **Indoors:** unknown **Seed germination:** fairly easy in a warm, moist medium; maximum of two months

Though it is smaller than the coconut palm, the Barbel palm is even more colorful. Young trees are very spiny.

## Acoelorraphe wrightii
### Everglades palm, paurotis palm

**Distribution:** Caribbean, southern Mexico, Central America, and northern South America in moist or swampy lowlands **Growth habit:** densely clustering **Height & width:** 20–40 ft. (6–12 m) tall, 15–20 ft. (4.5–6 m) wide **Trunk(s):** 15 ft. (4.5 m) tall, 4 in. (10 cm) thick; upper parts with a beautiful pattern of old leaf bases and dark brown to reddish brown fibers; older parts

dark gray with closely set rings **Crownshaft:** none **Leaves:** palmate, semicircular, 3 ft. (90 cm) wide, deeply segmented, light to deep green above, silvery green beneath, on stalks 3 ft. (90 cm) long and armed with hooked teeth **Flower clusters:** 3 ft. (90 cm) long, erect, and densely packed with tiny yellowish white bisexual flowers

*Acanthophoenix rubra,* a juvenile, in Florida.

Opposite: *Brahea edulis,* the Guadalupe palm, lines a path in California. Paul Craft

**Fruit:** round, ¼ in. (6 mm) wide, turning from orange to black when ripe **Growth rate:** medium; slow in dry conditions **Climate:** 9b through 11 in wet or dry climates, returns from the ground if frozen down in 9a or 8b **Exposure:** sun; can adapt to part shade **Soil:** humus laden **Water needs:** high **Salt tolerance:** medium **Indoors:** only with warmth and very intense light **Seed germination:** easy in a warm, moist medium; maximum of three months

Nothing is more beautiful than a mature, well-grown clump of this palm with its slender trunks of varying heights—the essence of the tropical look. Because each clump is clothed with leaves from top to bottom, this palm can be used as an isolated specimen in an expanse of lawn or to form a large hedge. Without a regular supply of moisture, however, the tree becomes unattractive. It even tolerates standing water.

## *Acrocomia aculeata*
### Macaw palm, gru-gru palm

**Distribution:** Caribbean Islands, through tropical Mexico and Central America to northern and eastern South America, in wet savannas and open places **Growth habit:** solitary **Height & width:** 15–40 ft. (4.5–12 m) tall, 10–15 ft. (3–4.5 m) wide **Trunk(s):** 15–35 ft. (4.5–10.5 m) tall, 1 ft. (30 cm) thick, white to nearly white, often with a bulge near the middle; young trunks always have spines, older ones may or may not **Crownshaft:** none **Leaves:** pinnate, plumose, 10 ft. (3 m) long, dark green, leaves and leaf stalks covered with spines 3 in. (8 cm) long **Flower clusters:** sprays 5 ft. (1.5 m) long

*Acoelorraphe wrightii*, in Florida.

*Acrocomia aculeata*, in Florida.

emerging from woody, spiny bracts and bearing yellowish unisexual flowers of both sexes **Fruit:** round, ½ in. (12 mm) wide, brown when ripe **Growth rate:** usually quite fast once past the seedling stage **Climate:** 10 and 11, usually surviving in 9b and sometimes in 9a depending on provenance **Exposure:** full sun; can adapt to part shade **Soil:** any but benefits from organic material or a mulch **Water needs:** medium, but survives in dry conditions **Salt tolerance:** slight **Indoors:** good with much space and intense light **Seed germination:** difficult; up to three years, even in a warm, moist medium

This very beautiful and even noble-appearing palm has strong visual affinities with all but the tallest royal palms. It is best used as a specimen tree in large gardens where its spines will not harm passersby.

*Adonidia merrillii*, inflorescence, in Florida.

## Adonidia merrillii
Christmas palm, Manila palm

**Distribution:** lowlands of the Philippine Islands **Growth habit:** solitary **Height & width:** 20–30 ft. (6–9 m) tall, 10–12 ft. (3–4 m) wide **Trunk(s):** 20 ft. (6 m) tall, light to dark gray to tan with closely set indistinct rings **Crownshaft:** 1–3 ft. (30–90 cm) tall, light to dark green, smooth, only slightly bulging at base **Leaves:** pinnate, to 9 ft. (2.7 m) long, strongly recurved, V-shaped in cross section, with stiff 1-ft. (30-cm) long leaflets that are deep green above and lighter green beneath **Flower clusters:** sprays 2 ft. (60 cm) long bearing whitish unisexual flowers of both sexes **Fruit:** oval, 1–1½ in. (2.5–4 cm) long, bright red when ripe **Growth rate:** medium **Climate:** 10b and 11, marginal in 10a **Exposure:** sun or part shade **Soil:** any but benefits from organic material or a mulch **Water needs:** medium, but grows faster with regular irrigation **Salt tolerance:** slight **Indoors:** good with enough light and space **Seed germination:** easy; one to three months in a warm, moist medium

The palm has a formal, architectural appearance. It looks good in groups of individuals of varying heights even planted in the middle of a lawn. It is especially wonderful in a patio or

*Adonidia merrillii*, in Sugarloaf Key, Florida. Paul Craft

*Adonidia merrillii*, fruit, in Florida.

other intimate site and is endearing in front of a contrasting background that allows its form and striking silhouette to be seen. It is prone to lethal yellowing, however, and very frost sensitive. The fruits turn red around the Christmas holiday.

## Aiphanes aculeata
### Ruffle palm, coyure palm
**Distribution:** foothills of the northeastern Andes **Growth habit:** solitary **Height & width:** 25–40 ft. (7.5–12 m) tall, 10 ft. (3 m) wide **Trunk(s):** 30 ft. (9 m) tall, 6 in. (15 cm) thick, dark gray to dark brown with widely spaced rings of short black spines **Crownshaft:** none **Leaves:** pinnate, plumose, 5–8 ft. (1.5–2.4 m) long, with numerous deep green leaflets 1 ft. (30 cm) long, each with a jagged end, all leaf parts covered with short black spines **Flower clusters:** globular "sprays" of small yellow unisexual flowers of both sexes **Fruit:** round, 1 in. (2.5 cm) wide, deep orange

*Aiphanes aculeata*, flowers and fruit, in Florida.

or deep red, in pendent clusters **Growth rate:** medium to slow in Mediterranean climates; medium to fast in tropical or nearly tropical climes **Climate:** 10 and 11 **Exposure:** full sun; can adapt to part shade **Soil:** humus laden and slightly acidic **Water needs:** high, but somewhat drought tolerant when established **Salt tolerance:** none **Indoors:** good with enough light, moisture, and air circulation **Seed germination:** difficult, taking up to a year unless the

hard outer coat is *carefully* removed, which will then necessitate using a sterile medium

The tree is exceptionally beautiful as a canopyscape. Its crown has one of the most visually satisfying shapes in nature, being full and round but with much contrast within the orb because of the jagged, plumose leaflets. It is unsatisfactory as an isolated specimen in lawns or other open spaces, even in groups of individuals of varying heights; it needs something at the bases of its trunks.

Strong winds make it unsightly and spininess can be a problem in certain landscape settings.

### *Aiphanes minima*
### Macaw palm

**Distribution:** West Indies, except for the island of Cuba **Growth habit:** solitary **Height & width:** 25–40 ft. (7.5–12 m) tall, 6–10 ft. (1.8–3 m) wide **Trunk(s):** similar to that of *Aiphanes aculeata* but taller, appearing thinner, and usually with more rings of spines **Crownshaft:** none **Leaves:** pinnate, shorter and not as plumose as those of *A. aculeata* with more and longer leaflets that have a distinct silvery cast beneath, each with a jagged end, all leaf parts covered with short black spines **Flower clusters:** globular "sprays" of small yellow unisexual flowers of both sexes **Fruit:** round, ½ in. (12 mm) wide, deep orange or deep red, in pendent clusters **Growth rate:** medium to slow in Mediterranean

*Aiphanes minima*, fruit, in Cuba. Paul Craft

*Aiphanes minima*, in Cuba. Paul Craft

*Aiphanes minima*, leaf crown, in Florida.

climates; medium to fast in tropical or nearly tropical climes **Climate:** 10 and 11 **Exposure:** similar to *A. aculeata* but needs more sun protection when young **Soil:** humus laden and slightly acidic **Water needs:** high **Salt tolerance:** none **Indoors:** good with enough light, moisture, and air circulation **Seed germination:** difficult, taking up to a year unless the hard outer coat is *carefully* removed, which will then necessitate using a sterile medium

This palm is exceptionally graceful and elegant with its full, rounded crown of pendent leaves. It is more aesthetically adaptable to specimen planting than is *Aiphanes aculeata*, especially in groups of three or more individuals of varying heights. Spininess may be an issue in certain sites.

## Allagoptera arenaria
### Seashore palm

**Distribution:** mostly beaches of southeastern Brazil but also just inland of the shore **Growth habit:** appears clustering because of several growing points at or just beneath the soil level **Height & width:** 8 ft. (2.4 m) tall, 10–15 ft. (3–4.5 m) wide **Trunk(s):** underground and not readily apparent **Crownshaft:** none **Leaves:** pinnate, plumose, 4–6 ft. (1.8 m) long, with many narrow, pendent, soft, ribbonlike leaflets that are 8–12 in. (20–30 cm) long, dark green above and silvery beneath **Flower clusters:** short spikes of closely packed small greenish yellow unisexual flowers of both sexes at the end of a stalk **Fruit:** round, 1 in. (2.5 cm) wide, yellow to orange, densely packed into a corncob-like cluster on stems 2–3 ft. (60–90 cm) long **Growth rate:** medium to slow **Climate:** 9 through 11, marginal in 8b **Exposure:** full sun; can adapt to part shade; one of the most wind-tolerant palm species **Soil:** sandy, never heavy, cold, or waterlogged **Water needs:** medium, but easily survives short periods of inundation as well as drought conditions **Salt tolerance:** very high **Indoors:** not good **Seed germination:** difficult; as long as two years

*Allagoptera arenaria*, in Florida.

*Allagoptera arenaria*, leaf, in Florida.

## Archontophoenix alexandrae
Alexandra king palm

**Distribution:** coastal rain forest of northern and central Queensland, Australia **Growth habit:** solitary **Height & width:** 30–50 ft. (9–15 m) tall, 15 ft. (4.5 m) wide **Trunk(s):** 25 ft. (7.5 m) tall, 1 ft. (30 cm) thick, gray to white **Crownshaft:** 4 ft. (1.2 m) tall, yellowish green to deep bluish green, smooth, slightly bulging at the base **Leaves:** pinnate, 6–10 ft. (1.8–3 m) long, sometimes up to 12 ft. (4 m), with many narrow leaflets that are 2–3 ft. (60–90 cm) long, deep green above, silvery beneath, the midrib twisting at midpoint so that leaflets at the outer half are vertically oriented **Flower clusters:** pendent sprays 2 ft. (60 cm) long bearing white unisexual flowers of both sexes **Fruit:** round, ½ in. (12 mm) wide, red **Growth rate:** medium to fast **Climate:** 10b and 11, marginal in areas of 10a with wet winters **Exposure:** part shade when young; full sun when older **Soil:** any but prefers organic material or a mulch **Water needs:** high **Salt tolerance:** low **Indoors:** good with much space and sufficient light, air circulation, and moisture **Seed germination:** easy; within one month

*Allagoptera arenaria*, fruit, in Florida.

As its common name suggests, this plant is one of the most valuable and most beautiful palms for seashores in warm temperate, subtropical, and tropical areas. It is easily grown in pots outdoors. Unfortunately, it is also slightly prone to lethal yellowing disease.

*Archontophoenix alexandrae* in Florida. Paul Craft

No palm is more regal and yet graceful than a mature specimen of this species with its straight-as-an-arrow, beautifully ringed, light gray trunk and massive crown of leaves. It is very difficult to transplant at any size, so choose a site with care. It does not do well where exposed to strong, dry wind, cold temperatures, or desert climes.

## *Archontophoenix cunninghamiana*
### King palm, bangalow palm

**Distribution:** Australia from coastal Queensland to southeastern New South Wales **Growth habit:** solitary **Height & width:** 50 ft. (15 m) tall, 15 ft. (4.5 m) wide **Trunk(s):** 40 ft. (12 m) tall, 1 ft. (30 cm) thick, light gray to light brown **Crownshaft:** 3 ft. (90 cm) tall, medium to dark green, slightly swollen at the base **Leaves:** pinnate, 8–10 ft. (2.4–3 m) long, with many closely spaced, mostly pendent leaflets that are 2–3 ft. (60–90 cm) long, medium to dark green above and paler green beneath, the midrib usually twisting at midpoint so that leaflets at the outer half are vertically oriented **Flower clusters:** numerous, branched, pendent spikes encircling the trunk just beneath the crownshaft and bearing small lavender, rose, or violet unisexual flowers of both sexes **Fruit:** round, ½ in. (12 mm) wide, pink or red **Growth rate:** medium to fast **Climate:** slightly hardier to cold than *Archontophoenix alexandrae* but somewhat less adapted to hot, humid summers **Exposure:** part

*Archontophoenix cunninghamiana*, in California. Paul Craft

*Archontophoenix cunninghamiana*, in Miami, Florida.

Archontophoenix cunninghamiana, fruit, in California. Paul Craft

Areca catechu at Montgomery Botanical Center in Miami, Florida. Paul Craft

shade in tropical or hot climates when young; full sun when older **Soil:** any but prefers organic material or a mulch **Water needs:** high **Salt tolerance:** none **Indoors:** good with much space and sufficient light, air circulation, and moisture **Seed germination:** easy; within one month

Many consider this species more desirable than *Archontophoenix alexandrae* because of its limper, more pendent leaflets and its great, colorful flower clusters. It is just as difficult as that species to transplant at any size, and does not do well where exposed to strong, dry wind, cold temperatures, or desert climes.

'Illawara', a form advertised as more cold tolerant than the species, has not demonstrated such hardiness in Florida, although it does seem to do better in sun.

## Areca catechu
### Betel-nut palm, betel palm

**Distribution:** original habitat unknown but probably Malaysia; now naturalized in all wet regions of the Asian tropics **Growth habit:** solitary **Height & width:** 50–75 ft. (15–22.5 m) tall, 15 ft. (4.5 m) wide **Trunk(s):** 40 ft. (12 m) tall, 8 in. (20 cm) thick; upper parts light to deep green, lower parts gray to tan; covered with light-colored, widely spaced rings **Crownshaft:** 3 ft. (90 cm) tall, bright green to yellow, smooth, slightly bulging at the base **Leaves:** pinnate, 6–8 ft. (1.8–2.4 m) long, arching, V-shaped in cross section, with many stiff, grooved, 2-ft. (60-cm) long leaflets that are deep green above and lighter green beneath **Flower clusters:** sprays 2 ft. (60 cm) wide bearing small fragrant yellowish white unisexual flowers of both sexes **Fruit:** egg-shaped, 1–2 in. (2.5–5 cm) wide, deep yellow to red when ripe, in pendent and heavy clusters **Growth rate:** fast to quite fast under optimum

*Areca catechu*, inflorescences, in Florida.

*Areca triandra*, in Hawaii. Paul Craft

*Areca catechu*, fruit of the yellow crownshaft form, in Australia. Paul Craft

conditions **Climate:** 11, survives in warm parts of 10b **Exposure:** full sun; can adapt to part shade **Soil:** humus laden and slightly acidic; benefits from a mulch **Water needs:** high **Salt tolerance:** none **Indoors:** good with enough light, space, moisture, and warmth **Seed germination:** easy and quick; maximum of one month in a warm, moist medium

The palm is too ethereal to be planted singly and isolated in the middle of space. Groups of at least three individuals of varying heights create a veritable symphony of form and color. Betel-nut palm is perfect as a canopy-scape.

## Areca triandra

**Distribution:** in low wet areas of eastern India, Southeast Asia, and the Philippine Islands **Growth habit:** mostly clustering; single-trunked plants are sometimes called *"Areca aliciae"* **Height & width:** 20–30 ft. (6–9 m) tall, 15 ft. (4.5 m) wide **Trunk(s):** similar to those of *A. catechu* but only about a third as thick and half as tall **Crownshaft:** quite similar to that of *A. catechu* but not as thick **Leaves:** pinnate, 6–8 ft. (1.8–2.4 m) long, arching, slightly V-shaped in cross section, with many, stiff, 2-ft. (60-cm) long, grooved, deep green leaflets, the terminal ones large and usually fused **Flower clusters:** small fragrant yellowish white unisexual flowers of both sexes in sprays smaller than those of *A. catechu* **Fruit:** egg-shaped, less than 1 in. (2.5 cm) wide, brownish orange to reddish brown, in heavy, pendent clusters **Growth rate:** medium to fast **Climate:** 11, survives in warm parts of 10b, resprouts from the ground if frozen down in 9b but succumbs to several successive winters which kill it back **Exposure:** part shade to full sun **Soil:** humus laden and slightly acidic; benefits from a mulch **Water needs:** high **Salt tolerance:** none **Indoors:** good **Seed germination:** easy and quick; maximum of one month in a warm, moist medium

Some individuals form dense clumps of stems and these look better if a few of the trunks are judiciously thinned out so that the beautiful form of the remaining stems may be more apparent.

## *Areca vestiaria*
### Orange collar palm

**Distribution:** low mountainous rain forest of eastern Indonesia **Growth habit:** mostly clustering, sometimes solitary **Height & width:** 10–20 ft. (3–6 m) tall, 15 ft. (4.5 m) wide **Trunk(s):** similar to those of *Areca triandra* but larger, with orange rings, and with prop roots at base **Crownshaft:** similar to that of *A. triandra* but colored with orange suffusion to solid deep orange or almost red; the form with maroon new growth has a brilliantly deep orange to red shaft **Leaves:** pinnate, 6–8 ft. (1.8–2.4 m) long, arching, slightly V-shaped in cross section, with many, stiff, 2-ft. (60-cm) long, deeply grooved, deep green leaflets, the terminal ones large and usually fused, midrib and stalk usually deep yellow to orange, some plants have intensely maroon-colored new growth **Flower clusters:** small fragrant orange unisexual flowers of both sexes in sprays smaller than those of *A. catechu* **Fruit:** egg-shaped, 1 in. (2.5 cm) wide, brownish orange to reddish brown, sometimes much deeper

*Areca vestiaria*, single-trunked form, in Florida.

*Areca vestiaria*, crownshaft and infructescences of single-trunked form, in Hawaii. Chuck Hubbuch

*Areca vestiaria*, in Australia. Paul Craft

*Areca vestiaria*, crownshafts, in Australia. Paul Craft

in color, in pendent and heavy clusters **Growth rate:** medium to slow **Climate:** 10 and 11 **Exposure:** part shade in hot climates; full sun in cooler climates; protection from hot, dry winds in all climates **Soil:** humus laden and slightly acidic; benefits from a mulch **Water needs:** high **Salt tolerance:** none **Indoors:** good **Seed germination:** easy and quick; maximum of two months There is hardly a more beautiful combination of form and color in the plant world, making this palm excellent for almost any landscape circumstance. It excels in close-up situations.

## Arenga caudata

**Distribution:** in forest undergrowth from Myanmar (Burma) through Thailand, peninsular Malaysia, Cambodia, Vietnam, and southeastern China **Growth habit:** densely clustering **Height & width:** 6 ft. (1.8 m) tall and wide **Trunk(s):** very thin and wiry **Crownshaft:** none **Leaves:** pinnate, 2–3 ft. (60–90 cm) long, leaflets 4–10, medium to dark green above, silvery beneath, linear to rhomboidal, the latter shape having irregularly incised margins and all but the ultimate leaflets having a tail-like projection at the end

*Arenga caudata*, in Florida.

Flower clusters: spikelike, usually hidden by the leaves, bearing white fragrant unisexual flowers of both sexes **Fruit:** ovoid, bright red, in pendent spikes **Growth rate:** mostly slow **Climate:** 10 and 11, successful in warmer Mediterranean climes if irrigated **Exposure:** part shade to nearly full shade, with protection from cold dry winds **Soil:** humus laden **Water needs:** medium **Salt tolerance:** none **Indoors:** very good **Seed germination:** fairly easy with warmth and moisture; two to four months; first leaf does not usually appear above soil for at least one month even though germination has occurred; *do not disturb during this period*

This palm is exquisite as a giant groundcover in partially shaded sites, as a specimen in a border, or alongside a path in the woods. It should be planted in an intimate setting to be seen, a requirement that can be difficult to achieve due to its small stature. The fruits of all *Arenga* species are an irritant to skin, so the trees must be carefully sited. Also, because the stems of all *Arenga* species die after flowering and fruiting, the trees should not be planted in areas that must be neat.

*Arenga engleri*, in Florida.

## *Arenga engleri*
### Dwarf sugar palm, Formosa palm

**Distribution:** low, wet mountainous forests of the Ryukyu Islands and Taiwan **Growth habit:** clustering **Height & width:** 15 ft. (4.5 m) tall, 8–15 ft. (2.4–4.5 m) wide **Trunk(s):** 10 ft. (3 m) tall, light gray to tan, usually covered in "woven" black stringlike fibers in all but the oldest parts **Crownshaft:** none **Leaves:** pinnate, 9 ft. (2.7 m) long, leaflets stiff, linear, 2 ft. (60 cm) long, thick, each with a jagged end, medium to dark green above, silvery beneath, midrib twisted near its midpoint so that leaflets at the outer half are vertically oriented **Flower clusters:** pendent sprays of yellow to orange fragrant flowers of both sexes **Fruit:** round, ½ in. (12 mm) wide, purplish black when ripe **Growth rate:** medium **Climate:** 9b through 11, marginal in 9a, good in Mediterranean climes if irrigated **Exposure:** part shade to high shade; tends to become yellowish in full sun of hot climates **Soil:** humus laden **Water needs:** medium **Salt tolerance:** slight

*Arenga engleri*, fibrous stems, in Mexico. Paul Craft

*Arenga engleri*, flowers.

*Arenga hookeriana*, in Florida.

**Indoors:** fairly good with adequate air circulation **Seed germination:** fairly easy in a warm, moist medium; two to four months; first leaf does not usually appear above soil for at least one month even though germination has occurred; *do not disturb during this period*

A large, well-grown specimen looks good isolated if the mass of trunks is judiciously thinned out to better reveal the appealing form of the stems. This palm is wonderful as a giant hedge as well as a centerpiece among lower-growing palms or other vegetation. Few palms look as good in containers. It is slightly prone to lethal yellowing.

## Arenga hookeriana

**Distribution:** in the undergrowth of monsoonal forests in peninsular Malaysia and southern Thailand **Growth habit:** densely clustering

**Height & width:** 3–6 ft. (90–180 cm) tall, 4–6 ft. (120–180 cm) wide **Trunk(s):** thin and wiry **Crownshaft:** none **Leaves:** pinnate, roughly diamond-shaped to nearly rectangular, unsegmented, 1–2 ft. (30–60 cm) long and 8–10 in. (20–25 cm) wide, light to deep emerald green above, distinctly silvery beneath, margins deeply lobed, each lobe with smaller incisions and ending in a short tail **Flower clusters:** 2 ft. (60 cm) long, erect and spikelike, bearing small yellow to orange unisexual flowers of both sexes **Fruit:** round, ¼ in. (6 mm) wide, bright red **Growth rate:** medium to slow **Climate:** 10b and 11, somewhat marginal in 10a **Exposure:** part shade to almost full shade, with protection from strong dry or cold winds **Soil:** any **Water needs:** high **Salt tolerance:** none **Indoors:** perfect **Seed germination:** fairly easy with warmth and

*Arenga pinnata*, in Cuba. Paul Craft

moisture; two to four months; first leaf does not usually appear above soil for at least one month even though germination has occurred; *do not disturb during this period*

This little gem of a palm is rare in and out of habitat. It is even choicer than *Arenga caudata* as a giant groundcover in partially shaded sites, in a border, or along a path in the woods. It may be a form of *A. caudata*.

## *Arenga pinnata*
### Sugar palm

**Distribution:** origin unknown; probably Indonesian rain forests **Growth habit:** solitary **Height & width:** 50–70 ft. (15–21 m) tall, 25–40 ft. (7.5–12 m) wide **Trunk(s):** 35–50 ft. (10.5–15 m) tall, 2 ft. (60 cm) thick, covered in all but the oldest parts by very thick and matted, strong black fibers with many 2-ft. (60-cm) long thin needle-like spines growing out of the fiber mass at many angles **Crownshaft:** none **Leaves:** pinnate, slightly plumose, mostly erect, 20–30 ft. (6–9 m) long, leaflets 2–3 ft. (60–90 cm) long, narrow, deep green above, silvery beneath **Flower clusters:** 7 ft. (2.1 m) long with many pendent branches bearing purplish unisexual flowers of both sexes **Fruit:** round, 2–3 in. (5–8 cm) wide, yellow when ripe **Growth rate:** fairly fast once

Arenga pinnata, stem and flowers, in Florida.

Arenga pinnata, fruit, in Florida.

past the seedling stage **Climate:** 10 and 11, survives in warmest parts of 9b **Exposure:** full sun; part shade when young **Soil:** any but benefits from organic material **Water needs:** high, but survives dry conditions when established **Salt tolerance:** slight **Indoors:** only with much space **Seed germination:** fairly easy with warmth and moisture; two to four months; first leaf does not usually appear above soil for at least one month even though germination has occurred; *do not disturb during this period*

The palm looks good in almost any site. It is large and spectacular enough to be sited alone surrounded by space, and it is magnificent as a large canopy-scape.

## Arenga tremula

**Distribution:** rain forest clearings of the Philippine Islands **Growth habit:** clustering **Height & width:** 15 ft. (4.5 m) tall, 8–15 ft. (2.4–4.5 m) wide **Trunk(s):** similar to those of *Arenga engleri* **Crownshaft:** none **Leaves:** pinnate, 9 ft. (2.7 m)

long, leaflets usually more widely spaced, limper, and pendent than those of *A. engleri*, light green above, distinctly silvery beneath, midrib twisted near its midpoint so that leaflets at the outer half are vertically oriented **Flower clusters:** tall spikes usually rising above the mass of foliage and bearing small greenish white to green unisexual flowers of both sexes **Fruit:** round, ½ in. (12 mm) wide, red **Growth rate:** medium **Climate:** 10 and 11 **Exposure:** part shade (where it will be more colorful) to full sun, with protection from cold dry winds **Soil:** humus laden **Water needs:** medium **Salt tolerance:** none **Indoors:** good **Seed germination:** fairly easy in a warm, moist medium; two to four months; first leaf does not usually appear above soil for at least one month even though germination has occurred; *do not disturb during this period*

More delicate and fernlike in appearance than *Arenga engleri*, this large palm serves the same landscape uses: as a canopy-scape or as an isolated specimen.

*Arenga tremula*, in Florida.

*Arenga undulatifolia*, in Australia. Paul Craft

## Arenga undulatifolia

**Distribution:** rain forest clearings of the Philippine Islands and Borneo **Growth habit:** solitary or densely clustering **Height & width:** 30 ft. (9 m) tall, 20 ft. (6 m) wide **Trunk(s):** similar to those of *Arenga engleri* but thicker **Crownshaft:** none **Leaves:** pinnate, 10 ft. (3 m) long, leaflets 2 ft. (60 cm) long, oblong, widely spaced, dark green above, silvery to white beneath, margins distinctly scalloped **Flower clusters:** sprays 2 ft. (60 cm) wide bearing small greenish white unisexual flowers of both sexes **Fruit:** round, 1 in. (2.5 cm) wide, brown **Growth rate:** medium **Climate:** 10b and 11, marginal in 10a **Exposure:** part shade to full sun, with protection from cold dry winds **Soil:** any including alkaline media **Water needs:** high, but tolerates dry conditions when established **Salt tolerance:** none **Indoors:** only with much space, bright light, and good air circulation **Seed germination:** fairly easy in a warm, moist medium; two to four months; first leaf does not usually appear above soil for at least one month even though germination has occurred; *do not disturb during this period*

*Arenga undulatifolia* is a vibrant-appearing species because of the shape of the leaflets and their silvery undersides that lend an air of movement to a clump even in still air.

*Arenga undulatifolia*, leaf outline, in Florida.

*Astrocaryum alatum*, in Australia. Paul Craft

*Astrocaryum alatum*, a juvenile tree, in Florida.

## Astrocaryum alatum

**Distribution:** southern Nicaragua, eastern Costa Rica, and eastern Panama **Growth habit:** solitary **Height & width:** 20–30 ft. (6–9 m) tall, 15–20 ft. (4.5–6 m) wide **Trunk(s):** 10–12 ft. (3–4 m) tall, 4–6 in. (10–15 cm) thick, indistinctly ringed and mostly covered in closely set rows of black spines **Crownshaft:** none **Leaves:** pinnate, 8–10 ft. (2.4–3 m) long, leaflets broad, 3 ft. (90 cm) long, grooved, grassy to deep green above, silvery beneath, on very spiny stalks 2–3 ft. (60–90 cm) long **Flower clusters:** clublike spikes emerging from large, paddle-shaped, woody, spiny bracts and bearing closely set yellowish white unisexual flowers of both sexes **Fruit:** round, 1 in. (2.5 cm) wide, yellow-brown **Growth rate:** medium to fast **Climate:** 10b and 11 **Exposure:** part shade to full sun; benefits from shade when young **Soil:** humus laden; benefits from a mulch **Water needs:** high, with high humidity **Salt tolerance:** none **Indoors:** good with sufficient space, moisture, and light **Seed germination:** difficult; as long as three years, even in a warm, moist medium

Few palm species can even equal this one's beauty, let alone surpass it, especially when

*Astrocaryum mexicanum*, in Florida.

*Astrocaryum mexicanum*, leaf stalks and flowers, in Florida.

young. Its leaves are almost unbelievably beautiful at all ages and create a unique tropical look in any garden. Young plants have fused leaflets that are broken into separate entities by strong winds. Beware of the very spiny stalks.

## Astrocaryum mexicanum

**Distribution:** tropical Gulf coast of Mexico, southern Belize, northern El Salvador, and northern coastal Honduras, in low mountainous rain forest **Growth habit:** solitary **Height & width:** 30–40 ft. (9–12 m) tall, 15 ft. (4.5 m) wide **Trunk(s):** 15–20 ft. (4.5–6 m) tall, 4–6 in. (10–15 cm) thick, indistinctly ringed and mostly covered in closely set rows of black spines **Crownshaft:** none **Leaves:** pinnate, similar to those of *Astrocaryum alatum* but slightly shorter with narrower leaflets **Flower clusters:** clublike spikes emerg-

ing from large, paddle-shaped, woody, spiny bracts and bearing closely set yellowish white unisexual flowers of both sexes **Fruit:** round, 1 in. (2.5 cm) wide, yellow-brown **Growth rate:** medium to fast **Climate:** 10b and 11 **Exposure:** part shade to full sun; benefits from shade when young **Soil:** humus laden; benefits from a mulch **Water needs:** high **Salt tolerance:** none **Indoors:** good with sufficient space, moisture, and light **Seed germination:** difficult; as long as three years, even in a warm, moist medium

Although unsurpassed as a patio or close-up subject, this palm is very spiny and should be sited carefully. It is excellent in the landscape when planted in group of three or more individuals of varying heights.

## Astrocaryum standleyanum
### Black palm

**Distribution:** lowland rain forest of eastern Costa Rica, Panama, and western Colombia **Growth habit:** solitary **Height & width:** 30–50 ft. (9–15 m) tall, 20 ft. (6 m) wide **Trunk(s):** 20–30 ft. (6–9 m) tall, 8–12 in. (20–30 cm) thick,

*Astrocaryum standleyanum*, in habitat in Costa Rica. Paul Craft

covered with closely set rows of 4-in. (10-cm) long black spines on all but the oldest parts **Crownshaft:** none **Leaves:** pinnate, plumose, 10 ft. (3 m) long, leaflets 2–3 ft. (60–90 cm) long, narrow, and pendent, with a spiny midrib, dark green above, silver beneath **Flower clusters:** clublike spikes emerging from large, paddle-shaped, woody, spiny bracts and bearing closely set yellowish white unisexual flowers of both sexes **Fruit:** round, 2 in. (5 cm) wide, yellow-orange to red, in pendent clusters 6 ft. (1.8 m) long **Growth rate:** medium to fast **Climate:** 10b and 11 **Exposure:** part shade to full sun **Soil:** rich, humus laden **Water needs:** high

*Attalea butyracea*, in Florida.

Salt tolerance: none **Indoors:** unknown **Seed germination:** difficult; as long as three years, even in a warm, moist medium

Magnificent at every stage of growth, this palm is covered with stout vicious spines and thus not recommended for areas with high traffic.

## Attalea butyracea

**Distribution:** northwestern South America **Growth habit:** solitary **Height & width:** 60–100 ft. (18–30 m) tall, 20–40 ft. (6–12 m) wide **Trunk(s):** young stems covered with old leaf bases and a 1-ft. (30-cm) thick mass of black fibers, making them appear 2 or even 3 ft. (60–90 cm) thick; old trees have much thinner trunks; dark gray to dark tan **Crownshaft:** none **Leaves:** pinnate, 30 ft. (9 m) long, leaflets 3 ft. (90 cm) long, midrib invariably twisted so that leaflets at the outer half are vertically oriented, crown erect when young, nearly full and rounded when older **Flower clusters:** long, narrow sprays emerging from giant woody bracts and bearing yellow mostly female flowers but with a few males in each cluster **Fruit:** oval, 2–3 in. (5–8 cm) long, yellowish brown **Growth rate:** slow to very slow to form an aboveground trunk but subsequently growing much faster **Climate:** 10 and 11, resprouts from the ground if frozen down in 9b **Exposure:** sun **Soil:** any **Water needs:** medium **Salt tolerance:** slight **Indoors:** not good **Seed germination:** difficult; several years, even in a warm, moist medium

Even in zone 9b it is common to see gigantic specimens of this palm with 30-ft. (9-m) long leaves springing straight from the ground, where the growing point was protected from frost.

## Attalea cohune
### Cohune palm

**Distribution:** from western tropical Mexico through Central America **Growth habit:** solitary **Height & width:** slightly larger in all parts than *Attalea butyracea* **Trunk(s):** young stems covered with old leaf bases and a 1-ft. (30-cm) thick mass of black fibers, making them appear 2 or even 3 ft. (60–90 cm) thick; old trees have much thinner trunks; dark gray to dark tan **Crownshaft:** none **Leaves:** pinnate, 30 ft. (9 m) long, leaflets 3 ft. (90 cm) long, midrib invariably twisted so that leaflets at the outer half are vertically oriented, crown erect when young, nearly full and rounded when older **Flower clusters:** long, narrow sprays emerging from giant woody bracts and bearing yellow mostly female flowers but with a few males in each cluster **Fruit:** oval, 2–3 in. (5–8 cm) long, yellowish brown **Growth rate:** slow to very slow to form an aboveground trunk but subsequently growing much faster **Climate:** 10 and 11, resprouts from the ground if frozen down in 9b **Exposure:** sun **Soil:** any

*Attalea cohune,* a juvenile tree, in Florida.

*Attalea cohune*, fruit, in Florida.

*Attalea humilis* at Montgomery Botanical Center in Miami, Florida.

**Water needs:** medium **Salt tolerance:** slight **Indoors:** not good **Seed germination:** difficult; up to several years, even in a warm, moist medium

The most widely planted *Attalea* species, this palm is also one of the largest and most impressive—some would say it is *the* most impressive palm. It dominates the landscape as few other palms can and has an almost irresistible appeal, even before it forms an aboveground stem.

## Attalea humilis

**Distribution:** eastern coastal Brazil **Growth habit:** solitary **Height & width:** 12–15 ft. (4–4.5 m) tall, 15 ft. (4.5 m) wide **Trunk(s):** only very old specimens attain a short stem of 3 ft. (90 cm) maximum **Crownshaft:** none **Leaves:** pinnate, 10–12 ft. (3–4 m) long, growing directly from the soil until very old, leaflets 2½–3 ft. (75–90 cm) long, narrow, closely set, grassy to deep green, vertical twist to the leaf **Flower clusters:** similar to those of the giant species but much smaller **Fruit:** similar to those of the giant species but much smaller **Growth rate:** medium **Climate:** 10 and 11, resprouts from the ground if frozen down in 9b **Exposure:** part shade, especially when young; full sun when older **Soil:** likes a richer and more organic medium than the giant species **Water needs:** high **Salt tolerance:** none **Indoors:** unknown but should be a good candidate with enough light and moisture **Seed germination:** difficult; up to several years, even in a warm, moist medium

This most beautiful "small" attalea is still rare in cultivation but has much potential as it becomes better known: its hardiness, like that of the giants, is unusual for a tropical pinnate-leaved palm species.

## Bactris gasipaes
### Peach palm

**Distribution:** unknown; probably rain forest clearings in Central America **Growth habit:** mostly clustering, sometimes solitary **Height & width:** 40–60 ft. (12–18 m) tall, 20 ft. (6 m) wide **Trunk(s):** 30–50 ft. (9–15 m) tall, 1 ft. (30 cm) thick, light colored with wide and widely

*Bactris gasipaes*, in Florida.

*Bactris gasipaes*, trunk, in Florida.

spaced dark bands or rings of short black spines **Crownshaft:** none **Leaves:** pinnate, plumose, 8–10 ft. (2.4–3 m) long, leaflets many, 2–3 ft. (60–90 cm) long, ribbonlike, soft, and pendent, deep green, midrib spiny **Flower clusters:** much branched, growing from woody, spiny bracts and bearing creamy unisexual flowers of both sexes **Fruit:** ovoid, 2 in. (5 cm) long, green turning deep yellow and then bright red when ripe, edible **Growth rate:** fast when given sufficient moisture **Climate:** 10 and 11, resprouts from the ground if frozen down in warm parts of 9 **Exposure:** sun **Soil:** any but better with organic material **Water needs:** high **Salt tolerance:** slight **Indoors:** not good **Seed germination:** fairly easy but slow, even in a warm, moist medium

Whether solitary or clustering, this palm is very beautiful. Solitary individuals resemble delicate royal palms when seen from any distance. Clustering specimens look good even when planted alone, surrounded by space. The tree is completely spiny.

## Bactris major

**Distribution:** southern Mexico through Central America, into northeastern South America **Growth habit:** densely clustering **Height & width:** 20–40 ft. (6–12 m) tall, 15–30 ft. (4.5–9 m) wide **Trunk(s):** 20–30 ft. (6–9 m) tall, 2 in. (5 cm) thick; with black spines on all but the oldest parts; deep green with white rings **Crownshaft:** none **Leaves:** pinnate, 6–8 ft. (1.8–2.4 m) long, leaflets closely set, growing in a mostly flat plane, grassy to deep green **Flower clusters:** sprays 2 ft. (60 cm) wide emerging from woody, spiny bracts and bearing greenish yellow flowers of both sexes **Fruit:** ovoid, 2 in. (5 cm) long, blackish purple **Growth rate:** medium **Climate:** 10b and 11, marginal in 10a, usually resprouts from the ground if frozen down in 9b **Exposure:** part shade to full sun **Soil:** any **Water needs:** high **Salt tolerance:** slight **Indoors:** unknown **Seed germination:** fairly easy but slow, even in a warm, moist medium

*Bactris major*, in Florida. Paul Craft

*Bactris major* is among the finest palms for a large hedge or screen and is exquisite as a free-standing clump or a strong, large accent in masses of other tropical vegetation. It is very spiny.

## Beccariophoenix madagascariensis
### Giant windowpane palm

**Distribution:** rain forest in Madagascar **Growth habit:** solitary **Height & width:** 25–40 ft. (7.5–12 m) tall, 25 ft. (7.5 m) wide **Trunk(s):** 15–30 ft. (4.5–9 m) tall, 12 in. (30 cm) thick, covered in all but the oldest parts with a mat of dark brown fibers **Crownshaft:** none **Leaves:** pinnate, 12–15 ft. (4–4.5 m) long, deep green above, grayish green beneath, leaflets 3 ft. (90 cm) long, narrow, fused together except at the base in young plants to create "windows" adjacent to the very short stalk, older plants have separate pendent leaflets with midrib invariably twisted so that leaflets at the outer half are vertically oriented **Flower clusters:** sprays 2 ft. (60 cm) long emerging from torpedo-like bracts and bearing yellowish white unisexual flowers of both sexes **Fruit:** ovoid, 1 in. (2.5 cm) wide, purplish brown **Growth rate:** fast when given adequate moisture **Climate:** 10b and 11, marginal in 10a **Exposure:** part shade to full sun **Soil:** any including sandy media **Water needs:** high **Salt tolerance:** none **Indoors:** good with bright light and adequate water but quickly outgrows most spaces **Seed germination:** easy with heat and moisture; maximum of three months

One of the world's most beautiful palms, this species resembles the coconut palm as well as the giant species of *Attalea*. It is exceptional even as an isolated specimen, especially when younger and exhibiting its "leaf windows." When mature, it is absolutely magnificent.

*Beccariophoenix madagascariensis*, leaf base fibers, in Florida.

*Beccariophoenix madagascariensis*, in Florida.

*Bismarckia nobilis*, in Florida. Paul Craft

## *Bismarckia nobilis*
### Bismarck palm

**Distribution:** savanna of Madagascar **Growth habit:** solitary **Height & width:** 40–60 ft. (12–18 m) tall, 20 ft. (6 m) wide **Trunk(s):** 40–60 ft. (12–18 m) tall, 12–18 in. (30–45 cm) thick, older parts dark gray to dark tan with indistinct rings or grooves **Crownshaft:** none **Leaves:** palmate, 10 ft. (3 m) wide, segmented to one-third the distance to the stalk, stiff, medium to deep green, on very stout, unarmed stalks 6–8 ft. (1.8–2.4 m) long **Flower clusters:** 3-ft. (90-cm) long tentacle-like, sparsely branched spikes bearing purplish to black flowers of one sex **Fruit:** round, 1½ in. (4 cm) wide, brown **Growth rate:** medium to fast once past the seedling stage **Climate:** 9b through 11, marginal in 9a **Exposure:** full sun **Soil:** any but excels in richer soils **Water needs:** medium, but drought tolerant when established **Salt tolerance:** slight **Indoors:** not good **Seed germination:** variable; 18 months maximum; primary root is a "sinker" which goes 12 in. (30 cm) deep, necessitating a container 18 in. (45 cm) deep

*Bismarckia nobilis*, unripe fruit, in Florida.

*Bismarckia nobilis*, leaf sheaths and ripe fruit, in Florida.

Bismarck palm is among the world's most impressive and beautiful species not only for its size but also for the outstanding coloration of most plants now in the market. It is an excellent large specimen plant in front of a dark background. The tree is difficult to transplant successfully, so site it carefully.

## Borassodendron machadonis

**Distribution:** rain forests of peninsular Malaysia and Thailand **Growth habit:** solitary **Height & width:** 50 ft. (15 m) tall, 20 ft. (6 m) wide **Trunk(s):** 30–50 ft. (9–15 m) tall, mostly covered in crisscrossing leaf bases **Crownshaft:** none **Leaves:** palmate, circular, 5–6 ft. (1.5–1.8 m) wide, divided into six large deep green segments, each one deeply incised at its end, on grooved, unarmed stalks 6–8 ft. (1.8–2.4 m) long with razor sharp margins **Flower clusters:** pendent and ropelike with small flowers on male trees, spikelike with much larger flowers on female trees **Fruit:** rounded with a flat side, 4–5 in. (10–12 cm) in diameter, purple to brown **Growth rate:** slow to medium **Climate:** 10b and 11 **Exposure:** part shade to full sun **Soil:** any but benefits from organic material **Water needs:** high, with constant high humidity for best appearance **Salt tolerance:** none **Indoors:** very good and very beautiful with sufficient moisture and light **Seed germination:** two to four months; primary root goes 8 in. (20 cm) deep, necessitating a container at least 12 in. (30 cm) deep

Still rare in cultivation, this palm is of exceptional beauty. If its needs can be met, it exhibits a very open crown of great, deep green, pinwheel-like leaves. Drought and dry wind, however, make it unsightly.

*Borassodendron machadonis*

*Borassodendron machadonis*, fruit, in Florida.
Paul Craft

## Borassus aethiopum

**Distribution:** savannas of tropical Africa **Growth habit:** solitary **Height & width:** 60–80 ft. (18–24 m) tall, 15–25 ft. (4.5–7.5 m) wide **Trunk(s):** 40–60 ft. (12–18 m) tall, 2–3 ft. (60–90 cm) thick, dark gray, usually with a bulge near the midpoint **Crownshaft:** none **Leaves:** palmate, 8–12 ft. (2.4–4 m) wide, deep green, on stalks 6 ft. (1.8 m) long **Flower clusters:** sparsely branched and pendent, bearing small flowers on male trees, 1-in. (2.5-cm) wide flowers on females **Fruit:** round, 6–8 in. (15–18 cm) wide, brown **Growth rate:** medium **Climate:** 10 and 11 **Exposure:** sun at all ages **Soil:** any **Water needs:** medium, but drought tolerant when established **Salt tolerance:** none **Indoors:** not good **Seed germination:** two to four months; primary root goes down 18 in. (45 cm), necessitating a container at least 24 in. (60 cm) deep

*Borassus aethiopum,* in Florida.

*Borassus aethiopum*, a juvenile tree, in Florida. Paul Craft

This massive palm is not for small yards. Mature trees are a dominant part of any landscape and are spectacular from a distance. As a canopy-scape, this palm is superb and very tropical looking.

## *Borassus flabellifer*
### Palmyra, toddy palm, lontar palm

**Distribution:** unknown; now naturalized in Old World tropics **Growth habit:** solitary **Height & width:** 60 ft. (18 m) tall, 25 ft. (7.5 m) wide **Trunk(s):** similar to *Borassus aethiopum* but with more adherent leaf bases **Crownshaft:** none **Leaves:** palmate, 8–12 ft. (2.4–4 m) wide, deep green, on stalks that are shorter than those of *B. aethiopum* and with many more leaves in the crown **Flower clusters:** sparsely branched and pendent, bearing small flowers on male trees, 1-in. (2.5-cm) wide flowers on females **Fruit:** round, 6–8 in. (15–20 cm) wide, brown **Growth rate:** medium to slow **Climate:** 10 and 11 **Exposure:** sun at all ages **Soil:** any **Water needs:** medium, but drought tolerant when established **Salt tolerance:** none **Indoors:** not good **Seed germination:** two to four months; primary root goes down 18 in. (45 cm), necessitating a container at least 24 in. (60 cm) deep

This palm is second in economic importance only to the coconut palm for people in undeveloped countries across its range. It is, however, slightly prone to lethal yellowing. Leaves of young trees may have bluish tints.

*Borassus flabellifer*, stem, in Florida.

*Borassus flabellifer*, a mature tree, in Florida.

*Brahea armata*, a juvenile tree, in California. Paul Craft

## *Brahea armata*
### Blue hesper palm, Mexican blue palm

**Distribution:** Baja California and northwestern mainland Mexico from sea level to 5000 ft. (1500 m) elevation, mostly in canyons with streams or creeks **Growth habit:** solitary **Height & width:** 30–60 ft. (9–18 m) tall, 15 ft. (4.5 m) wide **Trunk(s):** 30–40 ft. (9–12 m) tall, 18 in. (45 cm) thick, with closely set rings or grooves **Crownshaft:** none **Leaves:** palmate, circular, 6 ft. (1.8 m) wide, divided into 50 or so stiff bluish green to icy blue segments, on stalks 5 ft. (1.5 m) long edged with strong spines **Flower clusters:** great upward-arching, branched spikes of creamy bisexual flowers, typically extending well beyond the leaf crown and, in younger palms, sometimes reaching the ground **Fruit:** round, 1 in. (2.5 cm) wide, black when ripe **Growth rate:** fairly slow **Climate:** 9 through 11, marginal in dry parts of 8b **Exposure:** sun; loses coloring in shade **Soil:** any **Water needs:** medium with perfect drainage, but drought tolerant when established **Salt tolerance:** slight **Indoors:** not good **Seed germination:** easy; one to four months;

*Brahea armata*, a mature tree, in California. Paul Craft

*Brahea armata*, flowers, in California. Paul Craft

primary root is several inches long, necessitating a deep container

Although it is beautiful enough to be planted as a single specimen, blue hesper palm excels as a loud accent in a mass of vegetation, its bluish starburst of leaves lending an almost unmatched fillip to other forms and colors. It is stunningly spectacular in bloom. The highly desirable blue forms are not very adaptable to wet, humid regions.

## Brahea decumbens

**Distribution:** foothills of northeastern Mexico in limestone-based scrub **Growth habit:** clustering **Height & width:** 8 ft. (2.4 m) tall, 15 ft. (4.5 m) wide **Trunk(s):** as long as 6 ft. (1.8 m) but always reclining to some extent and often prostrate; dark and fibrous **Crownshaft:** none **Leaves:** palmate, mostly semicircular but occasionally circular, divided into many, long, stiff, pointed segments that are mostly green on very young plants but otherwise bright grayish green to bright silver to a pure, almost luminescent powdery blue, on stalks 2 ft. (60 cm) long with tiny spines near their bases **Flower clusters:** sprays 1 ft. (30 cm) wide bearing bisexual flowers **Fruit:** olive-shaped and of the same size, light brown when ripe **Growth rate:** slow **Climate:** 9 through 11, marginal in 8b **Exposure:** full sun; resents shade **Soil:** any including alkaline media **Water needs:** low; soggy soil is fatal as are wet, humid conditions **Salt tolerance:** slight **Indoors:** not good **Seed germination:** easy; one to four months; primary root is several inches long, necessitating a deep container

Although still rare, this small palm is desirable as a tall groundcover or as an accent in the

*Brahea decumbens*, in California. Richard Travis

cactus and succulent garden. The nearly unique color of its mature leaves is unexcelled.

## *Brahea edulis*
### Guadalupe palm

**Distribution:** Guadalupe Island off the northwestern coast of Baja California **Growth habit:** solitary **Height & width:** 35 ft. (10.5 m) tall, 12 ft. (4 m) wide **Trunk(s):** 30 ft. (9 m) tall, 18 in. (45 cm) thick, deep brown to dark gray, swollen at the base **Crownshaft:** none **Leaves:** palmate, semicircular to diamond-shaped, 4–6 ft. (1.2–1.8 m) wide, with grassy to deep green segments cut halfway to the juncture of the stout, 5- to 6-ft. (1.5- to 1.8-m) long stalk **Flower clusters:** arching, shortly branched spikes with small yellow bisexual flowers **Fruit:** round, 1 in. (2.5 cm) wide, black when ripe **Growth rate:** medium to slow **Climate:** 9 through 11, never in wet climates with freezing winters **Exposure:** sun **Soil:** any but grows faster in organic material **Water**

*Brahea edulis*, fruit. Paul Craft

*Brahea edulis*, in California. Barry Osborne

needs: medium to low **Salt tolerance:** medium to slight **Indoors:** not good **Seed germination:** easy; one to four months; primary root is several inches long, necessitating a deep container

Like blue hesper palm, the Guadalupe palm is beautiful enough to be planted as a single specimen, yet excels as a loud accent in a mass of vegetation.

*Brahea moorei*, in habitat in northeastern Mexico. Richard Travis

## Brahea moorei
### Dwarf rock palm

**Distribution:** oak-forested mountains of northeastern Mexico from 4500 to 6500 ft. (1350–1950 m) elevation **Growth habit:** solitary **Height & width:** 4–6 ft. (1.2–1.8 m) tall, 6–8 ft. (1.8–2.4 m) wide **Trunk(s):** mostly underground, occasionally aboveground a few inches **Crownshaft:** none **Leaves:** palmate, circular, 30 in. (75 cm) wide, with many deep segments that are mostly stiff but occasionally pendent at the end and a deep, glossy green above and intense chalky white beneath **Flower clusters:** erect, spikelike, and held above leaves, bearing tiny yellowish bisexual flowers **Fruit:** round, ¼–½ in. (6–12 mm) wide, purplish to black when ripe,

in pendent clusters **Growth rate:** slow **Climate:** 8b through 11 **Exposure:** part shade **Soil:** any including slightly alkaline media **Water needs:** low **Salt tolerance:** none **Indoors:** unknown **Seed germination:** easy; one to four months; primary root is several inches long, necessitating a deep container

Dwarf rock palm is still rare in cultivation, but so beautiful and hardy that, once it is seen, it should be in great demand.

## Burretiokentia hapala

**Distribution:** rain forest of New Caledonia **Growth habit:** solitary **Height & width:** 35 ft. (10.5 m) tall, 12 ft. (4 m) wide **Trunk(s):** 25 ft. (7.5 m) tall, 6 in. (15 cm) thick, deep green with

*Burretiokentia hapala*, flowers, in Florida.

*Burretiokentia hapala*, in habitat in New Caledonia.
Bryan Laughland

*Butia capitata*, in California. Paul Craft

widely spaced light tan rings **Crownshaft:** loose, yellowish green to dark green or brownish green **Leaves:** pinnate, 8 ft. (2.4 m) long, 3 ft. (90 cm) wide, leaflets 2–3 ft. (60–90 cm) long, emerald green, regularly spaced on very short stalks, leaf crown exceptional when young **Flower clusters:** sprays 1 ft. (30 cm) wide bearing yellowish white unisexual flowers of both sexes **Fruit:** ovoid, ½ in. (12 mm) long, reddish brown when ripe **Growth rate:** medium to fast **Climate:** 10 and 11 **Exposure:** part shade to sun **Soil:** humus laden **Water needs:** medium **Salt tolerance:** none **Indoors:** good with adequate air circulation **Seed germination:** easy; maximum of three months

The distinctly ringed, almost pure green trunks and the large leaves are more than exciting in the landscape and are as tropical looking as the palm world has to offer. This species is a marvelous candidate for up-close and intimate plantings as well as specimen groupings of three or more individuals of varying heights.

## Butia capitata
### Pindo palm, jelly palm

**Distribution:** savannas from southern Brazil to Paraguay **Growth habit:** solitary **Height & width:** 35 ft. (10.5 m) tall, 15 ft. (4.5 m) wide **Trunk(s):** 20 ft. (6 m) tall, 18 in. (45 cm) thick, covered in crisscrossing leaf bases except on older parts, which are light to deep gray with closely set semicircling ridges **Crownshaft:** none **Leaves:** pinnate, 8–10 ft. (2.4–3 m) long, greatly arched, usually recurved, V-shaped in cross section, with many narrow, pointed leaflets, deep green, grayish green, or silvery blue, on stalks 3–6 ft. (90–180 cm) long with stout protrusions on margins **Flower clusters:** sprays emerging from large, woody bracts and bearing tiny, yellowish unisexual flowers of both sexes **Fruit:** round, 1 in. (2.5 cm) wide, orange, edible **Growth rate:** medium **Climate:** 9 through 11 in wet climes, 8 through 11 in Mediterranean climes **Exposure:** sun; can adapt to part shade **Soil:** any **Water needs:** medium, but somewhat drought tolerant when established **Salt tolerance:** slight In-

*Butia capitata*, leaf bases, in California. Paul Craft

doors: not good **Seed germination:** difficult; as long as three years, even in a warm, moist medium

This outstanding landscape subject creates a truly tropical effect. Nothing stands out quite like it against the darker greens of other vegetation. The palm is beautiful enough to stand alone and surrounded by space. It is one of the world's hardiest feather-leaved species.

## ×Butyagrus nabonnandii
### Mule palm

**Distribution:** a garden hybrid between the queen palm (*Syagrus romanzoffiana*) and the pindo palm (*Butia capitata*) **Growth habit:** solitary **Height & width:** variable, depending on

×*Butyagrus nabonnandii*, in Florida.

*Carpentaria acuminata*, in Florida.

which species is used as the female parent and whether or not there has been back crossing **Trunk(s):** variable; generally taller than the *Butia* parent **Crownshaft:** none **Leaves:** variable but with characteristics of both parents, seldom as recurved as the *Butia* parent **Flower clusters:** similar to that of the *Butia* parent but larger and fuller **Fruit:** round, 1 in. (2.5 cm) wide, orange, not edible **Growth rate:** faster than its pindo parent, often on a par with its queen parent **Climate:** variable but usually as cold tolerant as the *Butia* parent and adaptable to wetter climes **Exposure:** sun; can adapt to part shade **Soil:** relishes a generally richer medium than does the pindo **Water needs:** high **Salt tolerance:** none **Indoors:** good with bright light and adequate air circula-

tion **Seed germination:** the cross produces only sterile seed but seeds from the original cross are easier and faster than those of the pindo

Individuals favoring the *Syagrus* parent are especially desirable as they are faster growing and the most tropical looking palms for nontropical areas.

## *Carpentaria acuminata*
### Carpentaria palm, carpy

**Distribution:** rain forests of the Northern Territory in Australia **Growth habit:** solitary **Height & width:** 50 ft. (15 m) tall, 12 ft. (4 m) wide **Trunk(s):** 30–40 ft. (9–12 m) tall, 6–8 in. (15–20 cm) thick above the bulging base; gray to light tan with widely spaced rings or ridges **Crownshaft:** 3–5 ft. (90–150 cm) tall, smooth, slightly bulging at the base **Leaves:** pinnate, 10–12 ft. (3–4 m) long, V-shaped in cross section, with many, narrow, 2-ft. (60-cm) long, arching, deep green leaflets **Flower clusters:** 3–4 ft. (90–120

*Carpentaria acuminata*, fruit, in Florida.

*Caryota gigas*, in California. Richard Travis

cm) long, pendent, much branched, growing beneath the crownshaft and bearing white unisexual flowers of both sexes **Fruit:** round, ½ in. (12 mm) wide, red when ripe **Growth rate:** fast to very fast **Climate:** 10b and 11, marginal in warmest parts of 10a **Exposure:** part shade when young, sun when older **Soil:** any **Water needs:** high; tolerates soggy conditions **Salt tolerance:** slight **Indoors:** only with much space, intense light, and good air circulation **Seed germination:** easy but slow; may take a year

With its relatively straight trunk, the carpentaria palm is elegance personified, and yet it is noble in size and appearance. It is beautiful as an isolated specimen surrounded by space and even more attractive in groups of three or more individuals of varying heights. It is stunning as a canopy-scape.

## Caryota gigas
### Giant fishtail palm

**Synonym:** *Caryota obtusa* **Distribution:** mountainous rain forests of northern India, Myanmar (Burma), northern Thailand, Laos, and southern China **Growth habit:** solitary **Height & width:** 50–70 ft. (15–21 m) tall, 20–35 ft. (6–10.5 m) wide **Trunk(s):** 40–60 ft. (12–18 m) tall, 2–3 ft. (60–90 cm) thick, light tan to nearly white with widely spaced darker rings or ridges **Crownshaft:** none **Leaves:** doubly pinnate (bipinnate), 15–20 ft. (4.5–6 m) long, 10 ft. (3 m) wide, triangular, with many large, fishtail-shaped, pendent, grassy to deep green leaflets **Flower clusters:** 12 ft. (4 m) long or more, much branched, and pendent, growing from the rings of the trunk starting near the top and continuing downwards, bearing unisexual flowers of both sexes with many clusters forming over a period of several years **Fruit:** round, 1–1½ in. (2.5–4 cm) wide, reddish brown when ripe **Growth rate:** medium to fast **Climate:** 10 and 11, including nearly frost-free Mediterranean climes **Exposure:** part shade when young; full sun when older **Soil:** rich and humus laden **Water needs:** high **Salt tolerance:** none **Indoors:** too large **Seed germination:** easy but slow; may take a year

One can only think of a very tall, massive tree fern when considering the landscape potential of this palm. It is large and beautiful enough to be a specimen plant. As a canopy-scape, it is most impressive, its incredibly beautiful leaf silhouette absolutely magical against the sky. Crystals in the flesh of the fruit are a skin irritant, and maturation of the fruit spells the death of this giant.

## Caryota mitis
### Fishtail palm

**Distribution:** India, Southeast Asia, the East Indies, and the Philippine Islands **Growth habit:** densely clustering **Height & width:** 20–30 ft. (6–9 m) tall, 15 ft. (4.5 m) wide **Trunk(s):** relatively thin with a maximum diameter of 6 in. (15

*Caryota mitis*, leaflets, in Florida.

*Caryota mitis*, in the Dominican Republic. Paul Craft

cm) **Crownshaft:** none **Leaves:** doubly pinnate (bipinnate), 8 ft. (2.4 m) long, 6 ft. (1.8 m) wide, triangular, on stalks 2–3 ft. (60–90 cm) long; leaflets 6 in. (15 cm) long, shaped like inverted triangles with three indentations, each with a jagged end **Flower clusters:** 2-ft. (60-cm) long sprays of pendent branches bearing whitish unisexual flowers of both sexes **Fruit:** round, ½ in. (12 mm) wide, blackish red when ripe **Growth rate:** medium to fast **Climate:** 10b and 11, marginal in warm parts of 10a, where it resprouts from the ground if frozen down but succumbs if it freezes in successive winters **Exposure:** part shade to full sun **Soil:** organic, humus laden **Water needs:** high **Salt tolerance:** none **Indoors:** only with much space and bright light **Seed germination:** easy but slow; may take a year

This species is most beautiful as a large element in masses of other vegetation, but is effective standing alone if sited as a focal point. It makes a very beautiful screen. Fruits are skin irritants, and the tree is slightly prone to lethal yellowing.

## Caryota urens
### Toddy palm, jaggery palm

**Distribution:** rain forests of Sri Lanka, India, Myanmar (Burma), and western Thailand into peninsular Malaysia **Growth habit:** solitary **Height & width:** 40–60 ft. (12–18 m) tall, 15–20 ft. (4.5–6 m) wide **Trunk(s):** 30–40 ft. (9–12 m) tall, 1 ft. (30 cm) thick, light to dark gray with very widely spaced darker rings **Crownshaft:** none **Leaves:** doubly pinnate (bipinnate), 12 ft. (4 m) long, triangular; leaflets narrow, shaped like inverted triangles, each with a jagged end; deep green; leaf crown extended along the upper 20 ft. (6 m) of the trunk **Flower clusters:** 10 ft. (3 m) long, much-branched, and pendent, bearing yellowish to brownish white unisexual flowers of both sexes **Fruit:** round, ½ in. (12 mm) wide, red **Growth rate:** medium to fast **Climate:** 10b and 11, marginal in 10a **Exposure:** part shade to full sun **Soil:** humus laden **Water needs:** high **Salt tolerance:** none **Indoors:** only with much space and intense light **Seed germination:** easy but slow; may take a year

*Caryota urens*, in flower and fruit, in Australia. Paul Craft

The toddy palm can be used as a lawn specimen or in a shrub border. The fruit flesh and sap are powerful skin irritants. Still, the sap is tapped in Asia to make sugar (jaggery), alcoholic beverages (toddy), and sago.

## Chamaedorea cataractarum
### Cat palm

**Distribution:** along rivers and creeks in rain forests of southern Mexico **Growth habit:** clustering **Height & width:** 6 ft. (1.8 m) tall, 8 ft. (2.4 m) wide **Trunk(s):** very short, each one forking at

*Chamaedorea cataractarum*, in Belize. Paul Craft

its base, 1–1½ in. (2.5–4 cm) thick **Crownshaft:** none **Leaves:** pinnate, 3–4 ft. (90–120 cm) long, with many, narrow, pointed, soft, slightly pendent, glossy, deep green leaflets **Flower clusters:** 1- to 2-ft. (30- to 60-cm) tall erect spikes bearing yellowish unisexual flowers **Fruit:** round, ½ in. (12 mm) wide, green turning red to black when ripe **Growth rate:** medium **Climate:** 10 and 11, sometimes successful in warm parts of 9b, resprouts from the ground if frozen down in 9a **Exposure:** shade to part shade; sun if given sufficient water **Soil:** any **Water needs:** high; tolerates constantly soggy conditions **Salt tolerance:** none **Indoors:** very good with bright light and regular moisture **Seed germination:** easy but sporadic; usually only two or three months but can take up to a year

Cat palm is used as a clump of contrasting foliage within a larger mass of vegetation or as a tall groundcover. Delicate and ferny in appearance, it lends a beautiful gracefulness to any site in which it is planted.

## *Chamaedorea costaricana*
### Costa Rican bamboo palm

**Distribution:** rain forests of southern Mexico and Central America **Growth habit:** clustering **Height & width:** 12–20 ft. (4–6 m) tall, 6–10 ft. (1.8–3 m) wide **Trunk(s):** 15 ft. (4.5 m) tall, 1 in. (2.5 cm) thick, dark green with distinctly lighter colored rings **Crownshaft:** no true shaft, only large, persistent greenish sheaths **Leaves:** pinnate, 4 ft. (1.2 m) long, with many 8-in. (20-cm) long, light to dark green leaflets **Flower clusters:** 3-ft. (90-cm) long branches bearing small yellow or orange unisexual flowers **Fruit:** round, ½ in. (12 mm) wide, black when ripe **Growth rate:** medium **Climate:** 10 and 11, including nearly frost-free Mediterranean climes, marginal in warm 9b, where it will usually grow back if frozen down **Exposure:** shade to part shade **Soil:** humus laden **Water needs:** high **Salt tolerance:** none **Indoors:** good **Seed germination:** easy but sporadic; usually only two or three months but can take up to a year

*Chamaedorea costaricana*, in California. Richard Travis

Few plants are as robustly graceful as a well-grown clump of *Chamaedorea costaricana*. It is among the finest landscape subjects for shade or partial shade, and it is simply superb as a patio specimen or as a large accent in masses of vegetation. The clumps are much more beautiful if judiciously thinned to allow the lovely trunks to show.

## Chamaedorea elegans
### Parlor palm, neanthe bella

**Distribution:** rain forests of southern Mexico, Guatemala, and Belize, from sea level to 4500 ft. (1350 m) **Growth habit:** solitary **Height & width:** 6–8 ft. (1.8–2.4 m) tall, 4–5 ft. (1.2–1.5 m) wide **Trunk(s):** ½–1 in. (12–25 mm) thick, light green with much darker rings **Crownshaft:** none **Leaves:** pinnate, 1½–3 ft. (45–90 cm) long, with narrowly oval, light to medium green leaflets **Flower clusters:** erect, branching near the ends, bearing tiny yellow unisexual flowers

**Fruit:** round, ¼ in. (6 mm) wide, black when ripe **Growth rate:** medium to slow **Climate:** 10b and 11 **Exposure:** shade to part shade **Soil:** humus laden **Water needs:** high **Salt tolerance:** none **Indoors:** outstanding, probably the world's most widely grown indoor palm **Seed germination:** easy but sporadic; usually only two or three months but can take up to a year

Delicate and elegant, parlor palm is unexcelled as an accent in shady borders. If expense is not a problem, it makes one of the most beautiful tall groundcovers. It is worth plunging pots of this palm into shady borders during the frostless seasons in almost any zone for the great beauty they lend to such areas.

## Chamaedorea ernesti-augusti

**Distribution:** rain forests of southern Mexico, Guatemala, Belize, and northern Honduras **Growth habit:** solitary **Height & width:** 6–12 ft. (1.8–4 m) tall, 2–3 ft. (60–90 cm) wide

*Chamaedorea elegans*, flowers, in Florida.

*Chamaedorea ernesti-augusti*, in Venezuela.
Paul Craft

Trunk(s): 5–10 ft. (1.5–3 m) tall, light to dark green with closely set, much lighter green rings Crownshaft: green Leaves: pinnate in form but usually unsegmented, medium to deep green, grooved, with deeply cleft ends resulting in a narrow heart shape Flower clusters: similar to those of *Chamaedorea elegans* but taller and with fewer branches Fruit: similar to those of *C. elegans* but slightly larger Growth rate: medium to slow Climate: 10b and 11 Exposure: shade to part shade Soil: humus laden Water needs: high Salt tolerance: none Indoors: perfect Seed germination: easy but sporadic; usually only two or three months but can take up to a year

This little palm is attractive as a single-specimen accent in masses of vegetation of a border; however, it is almost unsightly planted alone and surrounded by space, although it makes a nice silhouette. In groups of three or more individuals of varying heights, it is a lovely tableau of leaves and stems. Environmental conditions can separate the leaf segments.

## *Chamaedorea metallica*
### Metallic palm

Distribution: rain forest of southern Mexico Growth habit: solitary Height & width: 6–9 ft. (1.8–2.7 m), 3 ft. (90 cm) wide Trunk(s): ½ in. (12 mm) thick, dark green with closely set darker rings Crownshaft: greenish Leaves: pinnate, usually unsegmented, with a bluish or leaden cast and a highly polished sheen, grooved a dark pure green, with cleft ends resulting in a narrow heart shape Flower clusters: branching near the ends, bearing yellow unisexual flowers, male clusters pendent, female clusters completely erect Fruit: round, black, on an orange stalk Growth rate: medium to slow Climate: 10b and 11 Exposure: shade to part shade Soil: humus laden Water needs: high Salt tolerance: none Indoors: perfect Seed germination: easy but

*Chamaedorea metallica*, unsegmented leaf form, in Belize. Paul Craft

sporadic; usually only two or three months but can take up to a year

Because of its form and unique coloration, this little palm is unexcelled in the landscape. It is beautiful in silhouette and, planted in groups of individuals of varying heights, makes a shimmering mass of beauty and one of the most exquisite large groundcovers.

*Chamaedorea metallica*, segmented leaf form, in Belize. Paul Craft

## *Chamaedorea microspadix*
### Hardy bamboo palm

**Distribution:** scrubby forest of foothills in northeastern Mexico **Growth habit:** clustering **Height & width:** 12 ft. (4 m) tall, 8 ft. (2.4 m) wide **Trunk(s):** to 8 ft. (2.4 m) tall, often partially prostrate, ½ in. (12 mm) thick, dark green with widely spaced whitish rings **Crownshaft:** none **Leaves:** pinnate, 2 ft. (60 cm) long, leaflets widely spaced, narrow, somewhat S-shaped, deep green above, often silvery beneath **Flower clusters:** erect spikes of tiny, yellowish white unisexual flowers **Fruit:** round, ½ in. (12 mm) wide, deep orange or red when ripe **Growth rate:** medium **Climate:** 9 through 11, marginal in 8b where it returns from the ground if frozen back **Exposure:** part shade to part sun **Soil:** any **Water needs:** medium **Salt tolerance:** slight **Indoors:** very good **Seed germination:** easy but sporadic; usually only two or three months but can take up to a year

Hardy bamboo palm is wonderful as a screen or an accent in borders and other massed vegetation. Its remarkable architectural look is most

*Chamaedorea microspadix*, in Florida. Paul Craft

apparent when its trunks are thinned and pruned to varying heights. Under such conditions, its silhouette is extraordinarily pleasant.

## Chamaedorea radicalis

**Distribution:** oak forests of foothills in northeastern Mexico **Growth habit:** mostly trunkless, sometimes solitary **Height & width:** trunkless forms 5 ft. (1.5 m) tall, 6 ft. (1.8 m) wide; solitaries 12–15 ft. (4–4.5 m) tall, 4 ft. (1.2 m) wide **Trunk(s):** solitaries 12 ft. (4 m) tall, 1 in. (2.5 cm) thick, light green **Crownshaft:** solitaries have very light green shafts that are no wider than the trunks **Leaves:** pinnate, 3 ft. (90 cm) long, 2 ft. (60 cm) wide, leaflets 1 ft. (30 cm) long, medium green **Flower clusters:** 3- to 4-ft. (90- to 120-cm) long, erect spikes of small yellow to orange unisexual flowers **Fruit:** round, ½ in. (12 mm) wide, orange to red when ripe **Growth rate:** medium to slow **Climate:** solitaries in 8b through 11; trunkless forms marginal and resprouting from the ground in 8a **Exposure:** part shade to part sun **Soil:** any **Water needs:** medium **Salt tolerance:** none **Indoors:** good **Seed germination:** easy but sporadic; usually only two or three months but can take up to a year

Trunkless forms make choice large groundcovers. Solitary-trunked trees are uncommonly graceful and tropical looking and are simply superb in groups of three or more individuals of varying heights. Although they are wonderful as small canopy-scapes, they are not good when planted as isolated specimens.

## Chamaedorea seifrizii
### Bamboo palm, reed palm

**Distribution:** southern Mexico, Belize, Guatemala, and Honduras **Growth habit:** densely clustering **Height & width:** 12 ft. (4 m) tall and half as wide **Trunk(s):** 10 ft. (3 m) tall, dark green, indistinctly ringed **Crownshaft:** loose and indistinct **Leaves:** pinnate, ca. 2 ft. (60 cm) long, with broad to very narrow dark green leaflets ca. 8 in. (20 cm) long **Flower clusters:** erect,

*Chamaedorea radicalis*, aerial-trunked form, in Florida.

*Chamaedorea seifrizii*, narrow-leaved form, in Florida.

*Chamaedorea seifrizii*, broad-leaved form, in Florida.

*Chamaedorea tepejilote*, inflorescences, in California.

sparsely branched, bearing aromatic yellowish unisexual flowers **Fruit:** round, ¼ in. (6 mm) wide, black when ripe **Growth rate:** medium to fast **Climate:** 10 and 11, resprouts from the ground if frozen down in 9 **Exposure:** shade to part sun **Soil:** any including alkaline media **Water needs:** medium **Salt tolerance:** slight **Indoors:** good **Seed germination:** easy but sporadic; usually only two or three months but can take up to a year

This palm has a stiff but elegant aspect that is best used as an accent or silhouette indoors. Unpruned stems are densely clustered and usually provide a wall of leaves from top to bottom, but when the stems are judiciously thinned, the beauty of the silhouette is greatly enhanced.

## Chamaedorea tepejilote

**Distribution:** rain forests from southern Mexico to northwestern Colombia **Growth habit:** solitary and clustering **Height & width:** 15–25 ft. (4.5–7.5 m) tall, 10 ft. (3 m) wide **Trunk(s):** 10–20 ft. (3–6 m) tall, ½–3 in. (12–80 mm) thick, dark green with widely spaced, dark gray rings **Crownshaft:** loose and indistinct **Leaves:** pinnate, 5–6 ft. (1.5–1.8 m) long, leaflets broadly lance-shaped with long tips, medium to dark green **Flower clusters:** 2-ft. (60-cm) long pendent branches bearing yellow unisexual flowers **Fruit:** round, ½ in. (12 mm) wide, black when ripe **Growth rate:** medium to fast **Climate:** 10b and 11, marginal in 10a **Exposure:** shade to part sun **Soil:** any but relishes humus **Water needs:** high **Salt tolerance:** none **Indoors:** good **Seed germination:** easy but sporadic; usually only two or three months but can take up to a year

Because of its large, beautifully arching leaves (which must be protected from strong wind), it is among the most tropical looking species in the genus. It is unparalleled as a canopy-scape and is stunning in groups of three or more individuals of varying heights.

*Chamaedorea tepejilote*, in California. Paul Craft

## Chamaerops humilis
Mediterranean fan palm,
European fan palm

**Distribution:** rocky hills of the northern Mediterranean coast as well as foothills of North Africa **Growth habit:** mostly clustering, sometimes solitary **Height & width:** 6–20 ft. (1.8–6 m) tall, 6–30 ft. (1.8–9 m) wide **Trunk(s):** 3–20 ft. (0.9–6 m) tall, 1 ft. (30 cm) thick, covered in a dense mat of dark fibers and old leaf bases **Crownshaft:** none **Leaves:** palmate, semicircular to circular, 3 ft. (90 cm) wide, deeply segmented, grassy green to grayish green and even silvery, on stalks with strong, forward-pointing spines **Flower clusters:** short and much branched with small yellow bisexual flowers **Fruit:** round, ½ in. (12 mm) wide, orange to reddish brown when ripe **Growth rate:** slow to medium **Climate:** 8b through 11, marginal in dry parts of 8a **Exposure:** sun **Soil:** any including alkaline media **Water needs:** low, but grows faster with more water; not at its best in wet, humid conditions **Salt tolerance:** medium **Indoors:** not good **Seed germination:** easy; within three months but needs a container at least 6 in. (15 cm) deep

*Chamaerops humilis*, clustering form, in California. Paul Craft

*Chamaerops humilis*, single-trunked form, in Texas.

Solitary-trunked plants are best used as canopy-scapes but look unnatural as isolated specimens. Clustering plants are picturesque enough to be planted as isolated specimens, and old clumps create a tableau that is the essence of luxuriance and the semiarid tropical look.

## *Chambeyronia macrocarpa*
### Flame palm, red-leaf palm, red feather palm

**Distribution:** mountainous rain forest of New Caledonia **Growth habit:** solitary **Height & width:** 50 ft. (15 m) tall, 15 ft. (4.5 m) wide **Trunk(s):** 40 ft. (12 m) tall, 10 in. (25 cm) thick, greenish gray with widely spaced, lighter colored rings **Crownshaft:** 3–4 ft. (90–120 cm) tall, deep green, sometimes speckled with yellow streaks or entirely yellow, bulging at the base **Leaves:** pinnate, 10 ft. (3 m) long, recurved, with many, broad, leathery, grassy to deep green leaflets 3–5 ft. (90–150 cm) long, new leaves usually maroon to almost pure red **Flower clusters:** 1 ft. (30 cm) long, erect, much branched, with greenish white unisexual flowers of both sexes **Fruit:** rounded, 2 in. (5 cm) wide, deep red when ripe **Growth rate:** slow to medium; faster in wet, warm climes **Climate:** 10 and 11 **Exposure:** part shade when young, sun when older **Soil:** humus laden **Water needs:** high **Salt tolerance:** none **Indoors:** good **Seed germination:** easy; within three months

*Chambeyronia macrocarpa*, in Australia. Paul Craft

*Chambeyronia macrocarpa*, crownshaft. Paul Craft

Besides having gorgeously colored leaves, this palm has an even more beautiful form: a tall and straight light-colored trunk topped by a perfectly round crown of a few large and wonderfully arching leaves. It is unparalleled for up-close viewing. While it looks best as a canopy-scape, it is beautiful enough to stand alone.

### *Coccothrinax argentata*
### Silvertop palm, Florida silver palm

**Distribution:** southern Florida and the Bahamas **Growth habit:** solitary **Height & width:** 30 ft. (9 m) tall, 8 ft. (2.4 m) wide **Trunk(s):** 20 ft. (6 m) tall, 6 in. (15 cm) thick, upper part usually with matted dark fiber **Crownshaft:** none **Leaves:** palmate, circular, 3 ft. (90 cm) wide, deep glossy green above and silver beneath, on stalks 2 ft. (60 cm) long **Flower clusters:** erect and rising above the crown, with yellowish bisexual flowers **Fruit:** round, ½ in. (12 mm) wide, black when ripe **Growth rate:** slow **Climate:** 10 and 11, marginal in 9b **Exposure:** sun **Soil:** any including alkaline media **Water needs:** low **Salt tolerance:**

*Coccothrinax argentea*, in the Dominican Republic. Paul Craft

*Coccothrinax argentata*, in Florida.

*Coccothrinax argentea*, leaf crown and crownshaft, in the Dominican Republic. Paul Craft

excellent **Indoors:** not good **Seed germination:** easy; within three months but needs a container at least 6 in. (15 cm) deep

Silvertop palm works as a superb patio or courtyard tree for the seashore. It also makes an outstanding canopy-scape. The two-tone leaves are very alluring.

## Coccothrinax argentea
### Dominican silver thatch palm
**Distribution:** Hispaniola in grasslands and low altitude pinelands **Growth habit:** solitary, rarely clustering **Height & width:** 35 ft. (10.5 m) tall, 10 ft. (3 m) wide **Trunk(s):** 20 ft. (6 m) tall, 8 in. (20 cm) thick **Crownshaft:** none **Leaves:** palmate, 5 ft. (1.5 m) wide, deep green above, silver beneath, on stalks 5 ft. (1.5 m) long **Flower clusters:** short with yellowish white bisexual flowers **Fruit:** round, ½ in. (12 mm) wide, black when ripe **Growth rate:** medium to slow **Climate:** 10 and 11, marginal in 9b **Exposure:** sun **Soil:** any including alkaline media **Water needs:** low **Salt tolerance:** good **Indoors:** not good **Seed germination:** easy; within three months but needs a container at least 6 in. (15 cm) deep

The Dominican silver thatch palm is exceptionally beautiful because of the very open crown of perfect starburst-like round leaves with their shining silvery undersides.

## Coccothrinax barbadensis
### Barbados silver palm
**Distribution:** coastal areas of the Lesser Antilles and northernmost Venezuela **Growth habit:** solitary **Height & width:** 55 ft. (16.5 m) tall, 6 ft. (1.8 m) wide **Trunk(s):** 40 ft. (12 m) tall, 6 in. (15 cm) thick **Crownshaft:** none **Leaves:** palmate, circular, 3 ft. (90 cm) wide, deep green above, silver beneath **Flower clusters:** 2 ft. (60 cm) long, spikelike, with white bisexual flowers **Fruit:** round, ½ in. (12 mm) wide, black when ripe **Growth rate:** medium to slow **Climate:** 10 and 11, marginal in 9b **Exposure:** sun **Soil:** any including alkaline media **Water needs:** low **Salt tolerance:** good **Indoors:** not good **Seed germination:** easy; within three months but needs a container at least 6 in. (15 cm) deep

The tallest species in the genus, Barbados silver palm makes one of the most alluring canopy-scapes of any palm.

*Coccothrinax barbadensis*, in Florida.

## Coccothrinax crinita
### Old man palm
Distribution: Cuba Growth habit: solitary Height & width: 30 ft. (9 m) tall, 8 ft. (2.4 m) wide Trunk(s): 25 ft. (7.5 m) tall, 10–18 in. (25–45 cm) thick, depending on whether or not a covering of 1-ft. (30-cm) long dark fibers remains attached Crownshaft: none Leaves: palmate, circular, 3–5 ft. (90–150 cm) wide, dark, glossy green above, silvery green beneath, on stalks 4 ft. (1.2 m) long Flower clusters: 5 ft. (1.5 m) long, spikelike and arching out of the crown, with yellow bisexual flowers Fruit: round, 1 in. (2.5 cm) wide, black when ripe Growth rate: medium Climate: 9b through 11 Exposure: sun; tolerates part shade when young Soil: any including alkaline media Water needs: medium Salt tolerance: slight Indoors: not good Seed germination: easy; within three months but needs a container at least 6 in. (15 cm) deep

The shaggy trunk makes a great conversation piece but in humid areas can be ruined by strong winds.

## Coccothrinax miraguama
Distribution: coastal savannas and woods of Cuba Growth habit: solitary Height & width: 35 ft. (10.5 m) tall, 12 ft. (4 m) wide Trunk(s): 25 ft. (7.5 m) tall, 6 in. (15 cm) thick, upper part with a woven mesh design of fibers and leaf bases Crownshaft: none Leaves: palmate, circular, 3 ft. (90 cm) wide, dark green above, silvery green beneath, on stalks 4 ft. (1.2 m) long Flower clusters: 3 ft. (90 cm) long with yellow bisexual flowers Fruit: round, ½ in. (12 mm) wide, red turning black when ripe Growth rate: medium Climate: 10b and 11, marginal in warm parts of 10a Exposure: sun; tolerates part shade when young Soil: any including alkaline media Water needs: low Salt tolerance: some Indoors: not good Seed germination: easy; within three months but needs a container at least 6 in. (15 cm) deep

This species is generally considered the most beautiful in the genus. Its attractions are the wonderful crown of separated, round starburst-shaped leaves with their silvery undersides, the

Coccothrinax crinita, in Florida.

Coccothrinax miraguama, trunk, in Cuba. Paul Craft

*Coccothrinax miraguama*, leaf underside, in Cuba.
Paul Craft

beautiful design of the trunk fibers, and the colorful fruit. The grooves of the leaf segments create another beautiful shadow design within each leaf. The palm is unexcelled as a canopy-scape and is among the best close-up landscape subjects or silhouettes for patios, courtyards, and other intimate sites.

## Cocos nucifera
### Coconut palm

**Distribution:** original habitat unknown; probably coasts of the South Seas Islands **Growth habit:** solitary **Height & width:** 30–100 ft. (9–30 m) tall, 12–30 ft. (4–9 m) wide **Trunk(s):** 1 ft. (30 cm) thick, swollen at the base, white to tan with darker rings **Crownshaft:** none **Leaves:** pinnate, 8–15 ft. (2.4–4.5 m) long, 4–6 ft. (1.2–1.8 m) wide, with straight and somewhat stiff leaflets in young leaves but usually pendent in older ones, dark green to yellow-green, on stalks 3–5 ft. (90–150 cm) long **Flower clusters:** 5-ft. (1.5-m) long sprays of yellowish white branches bearing unisexual

*Coccothrinax miraguama*, in the Dominican Republic. Paul Craft

*Cocos nucifera*, in Florida.

*Cocos nucifera*, in Costa Rica. Nancy Landau

flowers of both sexes **Fruit:** ovoid, large and heavy, 1 ft. (30 cm) long, three-sided, green to yellow, orange, or brown when ripe, edible **Growth rate:** medium to fast **Climate:** 10b and 11 **Exposure:** sun **Soil:** any but faster and more robust growth in rich soil **Water needs:** medium **Salt tolerance:** great **Indoors:** not good **Seed germination:** easy but may take a year; entire fruit should be half buried in soil; will sprout unplanted if kept warm

The coconut palm is unsurpassed as a canopy-scape, and its silhouette is both stunning and a universally recognized emblem of the tropics. Unfortunately, it is prone to lethal yellowing. Tall coconut varieties are named for the locality in which they are found, while the shorter (dwarf) varieties are often named for the color of their immature fruit as well as their locality.

'Fiji Dwarf' is a slow grower with broad leaves and leaflets and green or bronze-colored fruit and petioles. It is not yet commercially available.

'Golden Malayan Dwarf', to 60 ft. (18 m) tall, has yellow-green leaves and golden fruit and petioles.

'Green Malayan Dwarf' is like 'Golden Malayan Dwarf' but with deep green leaves.

'Jamaican Tall', a tall, rapid grower, is very susceptible to lethal yellowing.

*Cocos* 'Maypan', in Florida.

*Cocos nucifera* 'Jamaica Tall', in Florida.

'Nino' is only 10 ft. (3 m) tall and has short leaves.

'Panama Tall', another rapid grower, has green or bronze-colored fruit and petioles.

'Red Spicata Dwarf' has a delicate appearance and orange-red fruit.

'Yellow Malayan Dwarf' is like 'Golden Malayan Dwarf' but with yellow leaves, fruit, and petioles.

*Cocos* 'Maypan', a hybrid between 'Malayan Dwarf' and 'Panama Tall', is intermediate in size and has leaves that are longer and broader than those of the species.

## *Copernicia alba*
### Caranday palm

**Distribution:** eastern Bolivia, Paraguay, northern Argentina, and southwestern Brazil, in monsoonal savannas **Growth habit:** solitary **Height & width:** 60–80 ft. (18–24 m) tall, 15 ft. (4.5 m) wide **Trunk(s):** 50 ft. (15 m) tall, 1 ft. (30 cm) thick, light gray to white, upper parts covered with crisscrossing old leaf bases **Crownshaft:** none **Leaves:** palmate, 3 ft. (90 cm) wide, deeply segmented, deep green above, silvery beneath, on stalks 4 ft. (1.2 m) long **Flower clusters:** 6–8 ft. (1.8–2.4 m) long, arching out of the crown, with short branches bearing yellowish bisexual flowers **Fruit:** ovoid, small, black when ripe **Growth rate:** medium to fast **Climate:** 9b through 11, marginal in 9a **Exposure:** sun **Soil:** any **Water needs:** medium, but adapts well to periodic flooding of fresh water **Salt tolerance:** slight **Indoors:** not good **Seed germination:** easy; primary root is long, necessitating a container at least 6 in. (15 cm) deep

This palm is noble, yet graceful. Its leaf crown is beautiful up close and from afar, and it works wonderfully as a canopy-scape. It is probably most picturesque in groups of three or more individuals of varying heights, simulating its colonial habit in the wild where great stands of the palm occur.

## *Copernicia baileyana*
### Bailey fan palm

**Distribution:** savannas and open woodlands of Cuba **Growth habit:** solitary **Height & width:** 50 ft. (15 m) tall, 18 ft. (5.4 m) wide **Trunk(s):** 40–50 ft. (12–15 m) tall, 2 ft. (60 cm) thick, columnar, white, and smooth **Crownshaft:** none **Leaves:** palmate, circular to diamond-shaped, 5 ft. (1.5 m) wide, with fairly shallow, very stiff segments that are deep green above, grayish green beneath, on stalks 3 ft. (90 cm) long with backward-pointing spines **Flower clusters:** 7 ft. (2.1 m) long, arching out of the crown, densely branched, bearing white bisexual flowers **Fruit:** rounded, 1 in. (2.5 cm) wide, black when ripe **Growth rate:** medium to slow **Climate:** 10 and 11 **Exposure:** sun **Soil:** any including alkaline media **Water needs:** medium, but drought tolerant when established **Salt tolerance:** slight **Indoors:** not good **Seed germination:** easy; primary root is long, necessitating a container at least 6 in. (15 cm) deep

*Copernicia alba*, in Florida.

*Copernicia baileyana*, leaf stalks, in Florida.

*Copernicia baileyana*, in Florida.

*Copernicia baileyana*, trunk and leaf crown, in Florida.

*Copernicia hospita*, in Florida.

A remarkable crown of large deep green rounded leaves with startling halo effect of stiff, comblike leaf segments, and the massive columnar trunk make this one of the world's most impressive species. It is eminently suited to specimen planting in large areas and is spectacular in groups of individuals of varying heights. It is slow, however, to reach its mature proportions.

## *Copernicia hospita*
### Cuban wax palm

**Distribution:** savannas and open woods of Cuba **Growth habit:** solitary **Height & width:** 20–25 ft. (6–7.5 m) tall, 15–20 ft. (4.5–6 m) wide **Trunk(s):** 20 ft. (6 m) tall, 8–12 in. (20–30 cm) thick, upper parts much thicker because of the persistent old leaf bases, lower parts dark gray to dark tan with circles of ridges **Crown-** shaft: none **Leaves:** palmate, semicircular to diamond-shaped, 5–7 ft. (1.5–2.1 m) wide, divided into deep, stiff grayish green to bluish green or silvery blue segments, on stout, armed stalks 5–6 ft. (1.5–1.8 m) long **Flower clusters:** 6–10 ft. (1.8–3 m) long, arching out of the crown, bearing bisexual flowers **Fruit:** round, 1 in. (2.5 cm) wide, black when ripe **Growth rate:** medium slow **Climate:** 10 and 11, marginal in 9b **Exposure:** sun **Soil:** any including alkaline media **Water needs:** medium, but drought tolerant when established **Salt tolerance:** slight **Indoors:** not good **Seed germination:** easy; primary root is long, necessitating a container at least 6 in. (15 cm) deep

The color of the leaves, especially in younger plants, makes this medium-sized palm extremely choice for patio or courtyard settings.

*Copernicia macroglossa*, in Florida.

## *Copernicia macroglossa*
### Cuban petticoat palm

**Distribution:** coastal savannas and salt marshes in Cuba **Growth habit:** solitary **Height & width:** 12–20 ft. (4–6 m) tall, 10 ft. (3 m) wide **Trunk(s):** 15 ft. (4.5 m) tall, 8–10 in. (20–25 cm) thick, dark gray to dark tan, with very closely set ridges; unless blown away or taken off, the shag of dead leaves reaches the ground and often renders the trunk as thick as it is tall **Crownshaft:** none **Leaves:** palmate, semicircular to wedge-shaped, 5–7 ft. (1.5–2.1 m) wide, dark green above, grayish green beneath, on very short stalks, resulting in a tightly packed leaf crown **Flower clusters:** arching spikes 6–8 ft. (1.8–2.4 m) long bearing yellowish bisexual flowers **Fruit:** round, ½ in. (12 mm) wide, black when ripe **Growth rate:** slow **Climate:** 10 and 11, marginal in 9b **Exposure:** sun **Soil:** any including alkaline media **Water needs:** medium, but drought tolerant when established **Salt tolerance:** great **Indoors:** not good **Seed germination:** easy; primary root is long, necessitating a container at least 6 in. (15 cm) deep

Cuban petticoat palm is dramatic and very distinctive in the landscape, where it may be used as a large accent in a wide border or an eye-catching focal point. Its character makes it adaptable to the cactus or succulent garden. A group of this palm is stunning if the individuals are of differing heights.

*Copernicia prunifera*, in Florida.

## *Copernicia prunifera*
### Carnauba wax palm

**Distribution:** low monsoonal areas of northeastern Brazil **Growth habit:** solitary **Height & width:** 40 ft. (12 m) tall, 12 ft. (4 m) wide **Trunk(s):** 30 ft. (9 m) tall, 10–12 in. (25–30 cm) thick, light tan to white, with prominent and distinctive spiral rings of stubby leaf bases usually on only the lower half of the stem in old plants **Crownshaft:** none **Leaves:** palmate, semicircular to nearly circular, 5 ft. (1.5 m) wide, with deep, stiff green to bluish green segments, on stalks 3 ft. (90 cm) long **Flower clusters:** 7 ft. (2.1 m) long, spikelike, and arching out of the crown, bearing dark yellow bisexual flowers **Fruit:** round, 1 in. (2.5 cm) wide, black when ripe **Growth rate:** medium **Climate:** 9b through 11 **Exposure:** sun **Soil:** any including alkaline media **Water needs:** medium **Salt tolerance:** some **Indoors:** not good **Seed germination:** easy; primary root is long, necessitating a container at least 6 in. (15 cm) deep

This moderately sized palm is wonderful in a large patio or courtyard, where the form of its trunk and large, rounded leaf crown may be appreciated. It looks especially good in groups of three or more individuals of different heights, and its silhouette is extraordinarily beautiful.

## *Corypha umbraculifera*
### Talipot palm

**Distribution:** probably southern India **Growth habit:** solitary **Height & width:** 60–100 ft. (18–30 m) tall, 20–40 ft. (6–12 m) wide **Trunk(s):** 50–70 ft. (15–21 m) tall, 3 ft. (90 cm) thick, upper parts covered with immense leaf bases somewhat resembling rhinoceros horns **Crownshaft:** none **Leaves:** palmate, circular, 20 ft. (6 m) wide on young plants, 10 ft. (3 m) wide on older plants, on armed stalks 10 ft. (3 m) long with very stout spines **Flower clusters:** the world's largest at 20–30 ft. (6–9 m) tall by 30–40 ft. (9–12 m) wide, pyramidal, growing atop the trunk, bearing millions of small yellowish white bisexual flowers **Fruit:** brown, 2 in. (5 cm) wide **Growth rate:** medium to slow when a seedling; medium after trunk formation

Climate: 10b and 11, marginal in 10a **Exposure:** sun **Soil:** any but appreciates fertile media **Water needs:** high **Salt tolerance:** none **Indoors:** not good **Seed germination:** fairly easy; within four months; needs a container at least 6 in. (15 cm) deep

Talipot palm is not only the most massive palm species but also among the most massive trees. Its slow growth when young and before it forms a trunk allows it to be used as a giant tropical-looking shrub and accent for many years. Some gardeners have it cut out as it begins to form a trunk since the inevitable outcome necessitates removing the trunks after they bloom and fruit. The life span of a single tree is from 30 to 80 years.

*Corypha umbraculifera*, flowers, in Panama. Paul Craft

*Corypha umbraculifera*, in Cuba. Paul Craft

Corypha utan, in Florida.

## Corypha utan

**Distribution:** northeastern India, Southeast Asia, and northern Australia to the Philippine Islands **Growth habit:** solitary **Height & width:** 50–70 ft. (15–21 m) tall, 20–30 ft. (6–9 m) wide **Trunk(s):** 40–60 ft. (12–18 m) tall, 2–3 ft. (60–90 cm) thick, covered with persistent leaf bases in a distinct spiraling pattern **Crownshaft:** none **Leaves:** palmate, circular, 10 ft. (3 m) wide, divided into very deep segments, on stalks 10 ft. (3 m) long **Flower clusters:** smaller than those of *Corypha umbraculifera* but pyramidal, growing atop the trunk, bearing millions of small yellowish white bisexual flowers **Fruit:** similar to those of *C. umbraculifera* but smaller **Growth rate:** medium to slow until trunk is formed **Climate:** 10b and 11 **Exposure:** sun **Soil:** any **Water needs:** medium to high **Salt tolerance:** none **Indoors:** not good **Seed germination:** fairly easy; within four months; needs a container at least 6 in. (15 cm) deep

Although the entire tree dies after fruits mature, it does not flower until it is 30 to 60 years old. This palm is slightly prone to lethal yellowing.

## Cryosophila warscewiczii
### Rootspine palm

**Distribution:** rain forest of eastern Costa Rica and northern Panama **Growth habit:** solitary **Height & width:** 30 ft. (9 m) tall, 15 ft. (4.5 m) wide **Trunk(s):** 20–30 ft. (6–9 m) tall, 6 in. (15 cm) thick, lower parts covered in twisting dark fibers and stiff, downward-pointing roots that look like spines **Crownshaft:** none **Leaves:** palmate, circular, 4–6 ft. (1.2–1.8 m) wide, with narrow, very deep segments that are deep green above, grayish green beneath, on stalks 6 ft. (1.8 m) long **Flower clusters:** compact sprays of white bisexual flowers **Fruit:** round, 1 in. (2.5 cm) wide, green turning bright white when ripe **Growth rate:** medium to slow **Climate:** 10 and 11 **Exposure:** part shade; tolerates sun when older **Soil:** any including alkaline media **Water needs:** high **Salt tolerance:** none **Indoors:** good **Seed germination:** easy; within a month; container needs to be at least 6 in. (15 cm) deep

Because of the large, perfectly circular leaves dancing in the full and rounded crown, there is

*Cryosophila warscewiczii*, in Costa Rica. Chuck Hubbuch

no more beautiful silhouette or canopy-scape. The tree is slightly prone to lethal yellowing.

## Cyrtostachys renda
### Sealing-wax palm, lipstick palm

**Distribution:** rain forest and swamps in Thailand, Sumatra, Malaysia, and Borneo **Growth habit:** clustering **Height & width:** 20–30 ft. (6–9 m) tall, 10 ft. (3 m) wide **Trunk(s):** 15–20 ft. (4.5–6 m) tall, 3 in. (8 cm) thick, upper parts green, lower parts light brown to light gray, covered with very widely spaced darker rings **Crownshaft:** 3 ft. (90 cm) tall, scarcely thicker than the trunk, smooth, deep orange to deep red **Leaves:** pinnate, 5 ft. (1.5 m) long, with widely spaced, narrow, emerald green leaflets, on orange to red stalks 1 ft. (30 cm) long, leaf

*Cyrtostachys renda*, growing in water, in Florida.

*Cyrtostachys renda*, crownshaft, in Florida. Richard Travis

*Dictyosperma album*, crownshaft, in Florida.

crown sparse and erect **Flower clusters:** greenish branches bearing white unisexual flowers of both sexes **Fruit:** round, ½ in. (12 mm) wide, black when ripe **Growth rate:** slow **Climate:** 11, marginal in 10b **Exposure:** part shade when young; full sun when older **Soil:** rich, humus laden **Water needs:** water lover, growing in submerged containers and soggy conditions **Salt tolerance:** slight **Indoors:** perfect with enough light, warmth, and moisture **Seed germination:** within three months when given constant high temperatures and moisture; seed is small

Because of its crownshaft, this species is considered by many palm collectors and aficionados the world's most beautiful species. It is hard to imagine a site in which it would not be the center of attraction, but it looks exceptionally beautiful when made a part of other vegetation.

## *Dictyosperma album*
### Hurricane palm, princess palm

**Distribution:** coastal forests of the Mascarene Islands **Growth habit:** solitary **Height & width:** 30–40 ft. (9–12 m) tall, 15 ft. (4.5 m) wide **Trunk(s):** 25–35 ft. (7.5–10.5 m) tall, 6 in. (15 cm) thick, gray to brown with closely set darker rings **Crownshaft:** 4 ft. (1.2 m) tall, smooth, white to green, bluish green, or reddish, swollen at the base **Leaves:** pinnate, 8–12 ft. (2.4–4 m) long, with narrow, deep green leaflets 2–3 ft. (60–90 cm) long; stalk of younger plants is often red **Flower clusters:** sprays 2 ft. (60 cm) long bearing yellowish unisexual flowers of both sexes **Fruit:** ovoid, deep purple to black when ripe **Growth rate:** medium to fast **Climate:** 10b and 11, marginal in 10a **Exposure:** part shade when young,

*Dictyosperma album*, in the Dominican Republic. Paul Craft

full sun when older **Soil:** any but appreciates humus **Water needs:** water lover **Salt tolerance:** none **Indoors:** only with space, good air circulation, and much water **Seed germination:** fairly easy; needs constant warmth and moisture; within two months

While good as an isolated specimen surrounded by space, this palm is incredibly tropical- and lush-looking when planted in groves or in groups of three or more individuals of varying heights. It withstands hurricane winds but is slightly prone to lethal yellowing.

Var. *aureum* has a yellowish orange crownshaft and leaf stalks.

## Dypsis baronii

**Synonym:** *Neodypsis baronii* **Distribution:** low mountains of northern and eastern Madagascar **Growth habit:** clustering, occasionally solitary **Height & width:** 25–30 ft. (7.5–9 m) tall, 20 ft. (6 m) wide **Trunk(s):** 15–25 ft. (4.5–7.5 m) tall, 6 in. (15 cm) thick, upper parts green, older parts gray, covered with widely spaced whitish rings **Crownshaft:** 1 ft. (30 cm) tall, sometimes up to 2 ft. (60 cm), yellow-green to white, smooth, slightly swollen at the base **Leaves:** pinnate, 6 ft. (1.8 m) long, slightly V-shaped in cross section, with grassy to dark green leaflets **Flower clusters:** sprays 2 ft. (60 cm) long bearing pinkish unisexual flowers of both sexes **Fruit:** round, ½ in. (12 mm) wide, yellow **Growth rate:** medium to slow **Climate:** 10 and 11, survives in warm parts of 9b **Exposure:** part shade to sun **Soil:** humus laden **Water needs:** medium to high **Salt tolerance:** none **Indoors:** only with bright light **Seed germination:** fairly easy; within three months

No landscape subject is more graceful than this palm. It should be planted against a contrasting background so that its diaphanous form can be appreciated. It is very choice when grouped as a clump in a patio or courtyard.

*Dypsis baronii*, stems, in California. Paul Craft

*Dypsis baronii*, in California. Paul Craft

*Dypsis cabadae*, in Florida.

## Dypsis cabadae
### Cabada palm

**Distribution:** rain forest of the Comoro Islands north of Madagascar **Growth habit:** clustering **Height & width:** 30–40 ft. (9–12 m) tall, 20 ft. (6 m) wide **Trunk(s):** 20–30 ft. (6–9 m) tall, 6 in. (15 cm) thick, green to grayish green with widely spaced white rings **Crownshaft:** 3–5 ft. (90–150 cm) tall, light to silvery green, slightly bulging at the base **Leaves:** pinnate, 8–10 ft. (2.4–3 m) long, arching, slightly recurved, slightly V-shaped in cross section, with stiff, narrow emerald green leaflets, on short stalks **Flower clusters:** 5 ft. (1.5 m) long, with yellow unisexual flowers of both sexes **Fruit:** round, ½ in. (12 mm) wide **Growth rate:** medium **Climate:** 10b and 11, marginal in 10a **Exposure:** sun; adapts to part shade when young **Soil:** any but appreciates humus **Water needs:** high **Salt tolerance:** none **Indoors:** only with intense light and much space **Seed germination:** fairly easy; within three months

Cabada palm's moderate size and gorgeous trunks make it one of the best patio or courtyard landscape subjects. It is wonderfully attractive in silhouette against a large wall of vegetation of contrasting color or form. As a canopy-scape, it is unsurpassed. The tree is slightly prone to lethal yellowing.

*Dypsis cabadae*, stems, in Florida.

## Dypsis decaryi
### Triangle palm

**Synonym:** *Neodypsis decaryi* **Distribution:** semi-arid low mountainous forest of extreme southeastern Madagascar **Growth habit:** solitary **Height & width:** 25–40 ft. (7.5–12 m) tall, 15 ft. (4.5 m) wide **Trunk(s):** 15–25 ft. (4.5–7.5 m) tall, 20 in. (50 cm) thick, light to dark gray with closely spaced grooves **Crownshaft:** none; live leaf bases create a triangular mass **Leaves:** pinnate, 10 ft. (3 m) long, growing from the trunk in three distinct planes, erect and stiffly arching, with narrow, 2-ft. (60-cm) long grayish green leaflets, on thick, wide stalks 1 ft. (30 cm) long **Flower clusters:** 3–5 ft. (90–150 cm) long with yellowish unisexual flowers of both sexes **Fruit:**

*Dypsis decaryi*, leaf bases, in Florida.

oval, 1 in. (2.5 cm) long, yellow to white when ripe **Growth rate:** medium to slow **Climate:** 10 and 11 in wet climes, marginal in dry parts of 9b **Exposure:** sun **Soil:** any including alkaline media **Water needs:** low, but grows faster and looks better with regular irrigation **Salt tolerance:** slight **Indoors:** not very good **Seed germination:** fairly easy; within three months

This sensational landscape subject is best sited against a dark green background where its great fountain sweep of grayish leaves is best displayed. Its silhouette is amazingly decorative. Triangle palm works well in almost any landscape but should not be crowded into a small space. It is slightly prone to lethal yellowing.

## Dypsis decipiens

**Distribution:** semiarid, plateau region of Madagascar from 4500 to 6400 ft. (1350–1920 m) elevation **Growth habit:** solitary, rarely clustering **Height & width:** 25–40 ft. (7.5–12 m) tall, 15 ft. (4.5 m) wide **Trunk(s):**

*Dypsis decaryi*, in Florida.

20–30 ft. (6–9 m) tall, 18–24 in. (45–60 cm) thick, with a bulge near the midpoint or at the base, light to dark gray with closely set lighter rings **Crownshaft:** 2 ft. (60 cm) tall, light green to nearly white, smooth, slightly bulging at the base **Leaves:** pinnate, 10 ft. (3 m) long, strongly arching, recurved, V-shaped in cross section, with stiff, erect, 2-ft. (60-cm) long, deep green to bluish green leaflets, on short stalks **Flower clusters:** sprays 2 ft. (60 cm) wide bearing yellow unisexual flowers of both sexes **Fruit:** round, ½ in. (12 mm) wide, yellow when ripe **Growth rate:** slow **Climate:** 10 and 11, marginal in dry parts of 9b **Exposure:** sun **Soil:** any, but best when planted high in wet climates **Water needs:** low **Salt tolerance:** slight **Indoors:** unknown **Seed germination:** fairly easy; within three months

This imposing plant works well as an isolated specimen or in groups of three of more trees of varying heights. It is visually arresting as a canopy-scape.

*Dypsis decipiens*, in California. Richard Travis

*Dypsis leptocheilos*,
trunk and crown-
shaft. Paul Craft

## *Dypsis leptocheilos*
### Teddy bear palm
**Synonym:** *Neodypsis lastelliana* **Distribution:** probably northeastern Madagascar **Growth habit:** solitary **Height & width:** 20–30 ft. (6–9 m) tall, 15 ft. (4.5 m) wide **Trunk(s):** 15–25 ft. (4.5–7.5 m) tall, 10 in. (25 cm) thick, light to dark brown with very wide white or nearly white rings **Crownshaft:** 2 ft. (60 cm) tall, only slightly wider than the trunk, covered in light to deep reddish brown felt **Leaves:** pinnate, elliptical, 12 ft. (4 m) long, with closely spaced dark green leaflets growing in a flat plane **Flower clusters:** sprays 2 ft. (60 cm) long bearing yellow unisexual flowers of both sexes **Fruit:** ovoid, 1 in. (2.5 cm) long, orange to brown when ripe **Growth rate:** medium **Climate:** 10b and 11, marginal in 10a **Exposure:** part shade to sun **Soil:** any including alkaline media **Water needs:** medium, but grows faster with regular irrigation **Salt tolerance:** none **Indoors:** only with much space and bright light **Seed germination:** fairly easy; within three months

This beautiful palm does not work well as an isolated specimen; it needs to be in groups of three or more individuals of varying heights or used as a canopy-scape. Old, tall specimens look much like straight-trunked coconut palms from any distance. In Florida, trees of this species are often misidentified as *Dypsis lastelliana*.

*Dypsis leptocheilos*, in Florida.

*Dypsis lutescens*, in El Salvador. Paul Craft

*Dypsis lutescens*, crownshafts and flowers, in Florida.

## Dypsis lutescens
Areca palm, golden cane palm, butterfly palm

**Distribution:** sandy riverbanks in eastern Madagascar **Growth habit:** clustering **Height & width:** 25–40 ft. (7.5–12 m) tall, 12 ft. (4 m) wide **Trunk(s):** 15–25 ft. (4.5–7.5 m) tall, 3 in. (8 cm) wide **Crownshaft:** 3 ft. (60 cm) tall, grayish green to silvery, smooth, slightly swollen at the base **Leaves:** pinnate, 6–8 ft. (1.8–2.4 m) long, arching and mostly recurved, V-shaped in cross section, with leaflets deep green above and silvery beneath, on yellow stalks 2 ft. (60 cm) long **Flower clusters:** sprays 2 ft. (60 cm) long bearing yellow unisexual flowers of both sexes **Fruit:** ovoid, 1 in. (2.5 cm) long, deep orange to black when ripe **Growth rate:** medium to fast **Climate:** 10b and 11, marginal in 10a **Exposure:** part shade or sun **Soil:** any **Water needs:** high **Salt tolerance:** none **Indoors:** easy but very prone to spider mite infestation **Seed germination:** fairly easy; within three months

*Elaeis guineensis*, trunk and fruit, in Florida.

No screen is more handsome than one made of adjacent clumps of this species. As a patio or courtyard subject, it is superb. It even looks good in the middle of a lawn surrounded by space. Like clumps of many other clustering palms, clumps of this species are more beautiful, especially as a silhouette, if judiciously and occasionally thinned.

*Elaeis guineensis*, in Florida.

## *Elaeis guineensis*
### African oil palm
**Distribution:** central and western tropical Africa **Growth habit:** solitary **Height & width:** 40–60 ft. (12–18 m) tall, 25 ft. (7.5 m) wide **Trunk(s):** 30 ft. (9 m) tall, 2 ft. (60 cm) thick, upper parts with wedge-shaped leaf bases, lower parts with rings of "knobs" **Crownshaft:** none **Leaves:** pinnate, slightly plumose, 15 ft. (4. 5 m) long, with dark green leaflets 3–5 ft. (90–150 cm) long, on viciously armed stalks **Flower clusters:** 1 ft. (30 cm) long, densely packed with flowers of one sex **Fruit:** oval, 2 in. (5 cm) long, black when ripe **Growth rate:** medium **Climate:** 10 and 11, resprouts in warm parts of 9b as long as growing point is underground **Exposure:** sun **Soil:** humus laden **Water needs:** medium to high **Salt tolerance:** none **Indoors:** not very good **Seed germination:** difficult; as long as three years, even in a warm, moist medium

The African oil palm is one of the few palms that look decent as an isolated specimen, so massive and spectacular is it. It is not for a small space.

## *Euterpe edulis*
**Distribution:** Atlantic coastal rain forest of Brazil to northern Paraguay and northern Argentina **Growth habit:** solitary, sometimes clustering

*Euterpe edulis*, in Lundkvist Palm Garden, Leilani Estates, island of Hawaii. Bo-Göran Lundkvist.

*Euterpe edulis*, in Brazil.

**Height & width:** 40 ft. (12 m) tall, 15 ft. (4.5 m) wide **Trunk(s):** 20–30 ft. (6–9 m) tall, 6 in. (15 cm) thick **Crownshaft:** 3 ft. (90 cm) tall, as wide as the trunk, deep green to orangish or reddish **Leaves:** pinnate, 10 ft. (3 m) long, with pendent dark green leaflets 3 ft. (90 cm) long, leaf crown semicircular **Flower clusters:** sprays of white unisexual flowers of both sexes **Fruit:** round, ½ in. (12 mm) wide, purple to black when ripe, edible **Growth rate:** medium **Climate:** 10 and 11 **Exposure:** part shade when young, sun when older **Soil:** humus laden and slightly acidic **Water needs:** high **Salt tolerance:** none **Indoors:** good with adequate space and moisture **Seed germination:** easy; 30 to 45 days in a warm, moist medium

Many consider this the most beautiful of all American palm species because of its diaphanous and exquisitely shaped leaf crown. It is stunning as a canopy-scape.

## *Euterpe oleracea*
### Assai palm

**Distribution:** rain forests of northern South America **Growth habit:** clustering but often takes a while to do so **Height & width:** 40–60 ft. (12–18 m) tall, 30–50 ft. (9–15 m) wide **Trunk(s):** 40–60 ft. (12–18 m) tall, 6 in. (15 cm) thick; upper parts dark green, lower parts gray, covered with widely spaced dark rings **Crownshaft:** 3–4 ft. (90–120 cm) tall, as thick as the trunk, green to light brown, smooth **Leaves:** pinnate, 8–12 ft. (2.4–4 m) long, slightly arching, with pendent dark green leaflets 3 ft. (90 cm) long **Flower clusters:** sprays 3 ft. (90 cm) wide bearing whitish unisexual flowers of both sexes **Fruit:** round, 1 in. (2.5 cm) wide, deep purple when ripe **Growth rate:** medium to fast **Climate:** 10b and 11 **Exposure:** part shade when young, full sun when older **Soil:** humus laden and slightly acidic **Water**

*Euterpe oleracea*, in Florida.

*Euterpe oleracea*, inflorescence, in Florida.

**needs:** very high; tolerates bogs **Salt tolerance:** none **Indoors:** only with much space, water, and humidity **Seed germination:** easy; 30 to 45 days in a warm, moist medium

No species is more beautiful and spectacular. It combines grace and nobility like few other things in nature and has an unequalled primeval beauty.

## *Euterpe precatoria*
### Mountain cabbage palm

**Distribution:** rain forests of Central America through all of northern South America east of the Andes, from sea level to 6500 ft. (1950 m) elevation **Growth habit:** solitary **Height & width:** 40–60 ft. (12–18 m) tall, 15–25 ft. (4.5–7.5 m)

*Euterpe precatoria*, in Australia. Paul Craft

wide **Trunk(s):** 30–50 ft. (9–15 m) tall, 10 in. (25 cm) thick, gray to white with widely spaced dark rings **Crownshaft:** 6 ft. (1.8 m) tall, as thick as the trunk, bright to deep green **Leaves:** pinnate, 15–20 ft. (4.5–6 m) long, slightly arching, bright green leaflets 3 ft. (90 cm) long and usually pendent, a few individuals have flat leaves with nonpendent leaflets **Flower clusters:** sprays 6 ft. (1.8 m) wide bearing yellow unisexual flowers of both sexes **Fruit:** round, 1 in. (2.5 cm) wide, purplish black when ripe **Growth rate:** medium to fast **Climate:** 10 and 11, including frost-free Mediterranean climes **Exposure:** sun to part shade **Soil:** humus laden and slightly acidic **Water needs:** high **Salt tolerance:** none **Indoors:** good with much space and moisture **Seed germination:** easy; 30 to 45 days in a warm, moist medium

This exceptionally beautiful palm has every virtue of the family except for bright coloration. It is attractive enough to be planted in almost any site, even as an isolated specimen, but is best when used as a canopy-scape or mixed in a wall of contrasting vegetation.

## *Guihaia argyrata*
## Chinese needle palm, Vietnamese silver-backed palm

**Distribution:** on limestone cliffs in southern China and adjacent northern Vietnam **Growth habit:** clustering **Height & width:** 8 ft. (2.4 m) tall and wide **Trunk(s):** 3 ft. (90 cm) tall, 6–8 in. (15–20 cm) thick, covered in dense, dark fibers, those near the top spinelike **Crownshaft:** none **Leaves:** palmate, circular, 3 ft. (90 cm) wide, with very deeply cut segments that are deep green above and chalky or bronzy white beneath, on stalks 3–4 ft. (90–120 cm) long **Flower clusters:** erect and broomlike with yellowish unisexual flowers **Fruit:** round, ¼ in. (6 mm) wide, black when ripe **Growth rate:** slow **Climate:** 9 through 11, marginal in dry parts of 8b **Exposure:** sun or part shade **Soil:** any including alkaline media **Water needs:** medium to low **Salt tolerance:** unknown; probably slight, if any **Indoors:** possible with intense light and good air circulation **Seed germination:** easy; within four months; needs a container at least 6 in. (15 cm) deep

*Guihaia argyrata*, foliage, at Fairchild Tropical Botanic Garden in Miami, Florida.

*Guihaia argyrata*, needlelike fibers of leaf crown, in Florida.

*Hedyscepe canterburyana*, in New Zealand. Bryan Laughland

This small, very colorful palm is ideal in a close-up or intimate setting. It also is perfect in containers.

## Hedyscepe canterburyana
### Umbrella palm, big mountain palm

**Distribution:** cloud forest on Lord Howe Island at elevations from 1200 to 2800 ft. (350–850 m) **Growth habit:** solitary **Height & width:** 35 ft. (10.5 m) tall, 12 ft. (4 m) wide **Trunk(s):** 25–35 ft. (7.5–10.5 m) tall, 1 ft. (30 cm) thick, gray with closely set dark brown rings **Crownshaft:** 2 ft. (60 cm) tall, 14–16 in. (36–40 cm) thick, light green to bluish green or whitish, cylindrical and smooth **Leaves:** pinnate, 8–9 ft. (2.4–2.7 m) long, erect and mostly recurved in older specimens, V-shaped in cross section, divided into stiff, rigid leaflets that are deep green above and paler green beneath, on stalks 1 ft. (30 cm) long **Flower clusters:** 3-ft. (90-cm) wide sprays of thick branches with white unisexual flowers of both sexes **Fruit:** oblong, 2 in. (5 cm) long, red when ripe **Growth rate:** slow **Climate:** 10 and 11 in cool Mediterranean climes, not in hot tropical ones **Exposure:** part shade to sun in cool climes **Soil:** humus laden and slightly acidic **Water needs:** high **Salt tolerance:** none **Indoors:** not good **Seed germination:** fairly easy; within three months

Architectural and formal appearing, umbrella palm is impressive in sites where its strong form or silhouette can be seen against the sky or contrasting foliage or structures. It looks good as a specimen planting, even surrounded by space in certain formal sites, but is better in groups of three or more individuals of varying heights.

## Heterospathe elata
### Sagisi palm

**Distribution:** Indonesia to the Philippine Islands **Growth habit:** solitary **Height & width:** 40–60 ft. (12–18 m) tall, 15 ft. (4.5 m) wide **Trunk(s):**

*Heterospathe elata* at Montgomery Botanical Center, Miami, Florida.

30–50 ft. (9–15 m) tall, 10–12 in. (25–30 cm) thick, light gray with widely spaced dark rings, seldom straight **Crownshaft:** none **Leaves:** pinnate, 6–10 ft. (1.8–3 m) long, only slightly arching, with somewhat pendent dark green leaflets 2 ft. (60 cm) long, midrib twisted so that leaflets at the outer half are vertically oriented, new growth usually reddish bronze **Flower clusters:** spikes 4 ft. (1.2 m) long bearing yellow to orange or white unisexual flowers of both sexes **Fruit:** round, ½ in. (12 mm) wide, white when ripe **Growth rate:** slow as a juvenile, medium to fast thereafter **Climate:** 10b and 11 **Exposure:** part shade when young; full sun when older **Soil:** humus laden **Water needs:** high **Salt tolerance:** none **Indoors:** only with space, bright light, and much water **Seed germination:** somewhat temperamental; within three months, if at all

This species has many similarities to the coconut palm. It is beautiful enough to stand as an isolated specimen but looks better in groups of three or more individuals of varying heights. It has a silhouette almost as beautiful as that of the coconut palm and is stunning as a canopy-scape.

## *Howea belmoreana*
### Sentry palm

**Distribution:** Lord Howe Island **Growth habit:** solitary **Height & width:** 20–30 ft. (6–9 m) tall, 10 ft. (3 m) wide **Trunk(s):** 30–40 ft. (9–12 m) tall, 6 in. (15 cm) thick, light brown to gray with closely set dark rings **Crownshaft:** none **Leaves:** pinnate, 7–10 ft. (2.1–3 m) long, strongly recurved, V-shaped in cross section, divided into stiff, erect, dark green leaflets 3 ft. (90 cm) long, on arching stalks 3 ft. (90 cm) long; **Flower clusters:** 6-ft. (1.8-m) long unbranched, tail-like spikes with tiny yellow to tan unisexual flowers of both sexes **Fruit:** oval, 2 in. (5 cm) long, reddish brown when ripe **Growth rate:** slow **Climate:** 10b and 11, marginal in wet parts of 10a **Exposure:** part shade in hot climes, sun in cool

*Heterospathe elata*, reddish new leaf, in Florida.

*Howea belmoreana*, in California. Barry Osborne

but frost-free Mediterranean climes **Soil:** humus laden or with a heavy mulch **Water needs:** medium **Salt tolerance:** none **Indoors:** good with adequate air circulation **Seed germination:** not easy; may take two years

With its striking architectural aspect, sentry palm is unsurpassed for a silhouette display against the sky, large walls, or contrasting vegetation colors. It also makes a good canopyscape.

## Howea forsteriana
### Kentia palm

**Distribution:** low elevations of Lord Howe Island **Growth habit:** solitary **Height & width:** 50–70 ft. (15–21 m) tall, 20 ft. (6 m) wide **Trunk(s):** 30–60 ft. (9–18 m) tall, 6–10 in. (15–25 cm) thick, dark green to gray with lighter rings **Crownshaft:** none **Leaves:** pinnate, 8–12 ft. (2.4–4 m) long, arching, divided into pendent, dark green leaflets 2–3 ft. (60–90 cm) long, on stalks 4–5 ft. (1.2–1.5

m) long **Flower clusters:** 6-ft. (1.8-m) long unbranched, tail-like spikes with tiny yellow to tan unisexual flowers of both sexes **Fruit:** oval, 2 in. (5 cm) long, orange or red when ripe **Growth rate:** slow, especially when young, slightly faster thereafter **Climate:** 10 and 11, marginal in dry parts of 9b **Exposure:** part shade in hot climes to full sun in cool climes **Soil:** any but best with humus or a mulch **Water needs:** medium **Salt tolerance:** some **Indoors:** perfect **Seed germination:** not easy; may take two years

Young plants have an astoundingly graceful and attractive fountainlike aspect, and there is likely nothing more elegant in all nature than these wonderful curves accented by the great

*Howea forsteriana*, fruit, in California. Paul Craft

*Howea forsteriana*, in California. Barry Osborne

drooping leaflets. It is one of the few tall palms that is beautiful enough to stand alone as an isolated specimen, but it is even more choice in groups of three or more individuals of varying heights. It makes a durable indoor plant.

## Hydriastele costata

**Synonym:** *Gulubia costata* **Distribution:** rain forests of Indonesia, New Guinea, and northeastern Australia **Growth habit:** solitary **Height & width:** 50–70 ft. (15–21 m) tall, 25 ft. (7.5 m) wide **Trunk(s):** 40–60 ft. (12–18 m) tall, 2 ft. (60 cm) thick **Crownshaft:** 4–5 ft. (1.2–1.5 m) tall, dark green, smooth, slightly bulging at the base **Leaves:** pinnate, 12–15 ft. (4–4.5 m) long, unarching, with many completely pendent, dark green leaflets 3–4 ft. (90–120 cm) long, leaf crown is hemispherical **Flower clusters:** 4–5 ft. (1.2–1.5 m) long with orange unisexual flowers of both sexes **Fruit:** oval, 3 in. (8 cm) long, bluish gray with white stripes **Growth rate:** medium to slow as a juvenile, fast thereafter **Climate:** 10b and 11 **Exposure:** part shade when young; full sun when older **Soil:** any but looks better

*Hydriastele costata,* in Florida.

and grows faster in humus-laden media **Water needs**: high **Salt tolerance**: none **Indoors**: only with space, intense light, and much water **Seed germination**: easy; within one month when given warmth and moisture

This exquisite species stands out in the landscape. It is incomparably spectacular because of its great stiff, curtainlike leaves. As a canopyscape, it is matchless. Groups of three or more individuals of varying heights create an irresistible tableau of tropical beauty.

## Hyophorbe indica

**Distribution**: wet forests on Réunion Island in the Indian Ocean **Growth habit**: solitary **Height & width**: 30–40 ft. (9–12 m) tall, 12 ft. (4 m) wide **Trunk(s)**: 20–30 ft. (6–9 m) tall, 8 in. (20 cm) thick, light gray with widely spaced dark rings **Crownshaft**: 2–3 ft. (60–90 cm) tall, light to dark green or light to reddish brown to nearly black, smooth, bulging at the base **Leaves**: pinnate, 6–8 ft. (1.8–2.4 m) long, slightly arching, divided into dark green leaflets 2 ft. (60 cm) long and growing in a flat plane in younger trees but growing at angles in older trees **Flower clusters**: sprays 3 ft. (90 cm) wide emerging from long, upward-pointing, hornlike bracts on the upper part of the trunk and bearing yellow unisexual flowers of both sexes **Fruit**: round, 1 in. (2.5 cm) wide, red when ripe **Growth rate**: medium to fast **Climate**: 10b and 11, marginal in warmest parts of 10a **Exposure**: part shade to sun **Soil**: humus laden and slightly acidic; benefits from a mulch **Water needs**: medium to high **Salt tolerance**: none **Indoors**: good with space, intense light, and adequate air circulation

*Hyophorbe indica*, in Florida.

**Seed germination:** fairly easy but can take as long as two years

This palm makes an attractive canopy-scape and is more than beautiful in groups of three or more trees of varying heights.

## Hyophorbe lagenicaulis
### Bottle palm

**Distribution:** scrub forests and savannas of the Mascarene Islands **Growth habit:** solitary **Height & width:** 20–30 ft. (6–9 m) tall, 8 ft. (2.4 m) wide **Trunk(s):** 15–20 ft. (4.5–6 m) tall, 2 ft. (60 cm) thick in lower part, tapering (sometimes abruptly) to 8–10 in. (20–25 cm) thick in upper part, gray to white with closely set rings or ridges **Crownshaft:** 2–3 ft. (60–90 cm) tall, mint green, smooth, bulbous at the base and often abruptly tapering to 8 in. (20 cm) near the top **Leaves:** pinnate, 6–12 ft. (1.8–4 m) long, greatly arching, strongly recurved, V-shaped in cross section, divided into erect, rigid, deep green leaflets 2 ft. (60 cm) long **Flower clusters:** sprays 3 ft. (90 cm) wide emerging from long, upward-pointing, hornlike bracts on the upper part of the trunk and bearing yellow unisexual flowers of both sexes **Fruit:** round, 1 in. (2.5 cm) wide, black when ripe **Growth rate:** slow as a juvenile, medium thereafter **Climate:** 10b and 11, marginal in warmest parts of 10a **Exposure:** part shade to sun **Soil:** any **Water needs:** medium **Salt tolerance:** none **Indoors:** good with intense light and adequate space **Seed germination:** fairly easy but can take as long as two years

Although the crowns are beautiful and dramatically architectural, the trunks are an acquired taste. Where they are planted would seem to make all the difference as to whether they are pleasing in the landscape: rather than trying to hide their unusual form, the latter should be accented.

## Hyophorbe verschaffeltii
### Spindle palm

**Distribution:** scrub forests and savannas of the Mascarene Islands **Growth habit:** solitary **Height & width:** 30–40 ft. (9–12 m) tall, 10 ft. (3 m) wide **Trunk(s):** 20–30 ft. (6–9 m) tall, 10–18 in. (25–45 cm) wide, spindle-shaped, the opposite shape of *Hyophorbe lagenicaulis* **Crownshaft:** 2–3 ft. (60–90 cm) tall, bluish green, smooth, swollen at the base **Leaves:** pinnate, 6–10 ft. (1.8–3 m) long, arched and recurved, V-shaped in cross section, with erect, rigid, dark green leaflets 2 ft. (60 cm) long **Flower clusters:** sprays 3 ft. (90 cm) wide emerging from long, upward-pointing, hornlike bracts on the upper part of the trunk and bearing yellow unisexual flowers of both sexes **Fruit:** round, 1 in. (2.5 cm) wide, black when ripe **Growth rate:** somewhat faster than *H. lagenicaulis* **Climate:** 10 and 11, slightly less tender to cold than *H. lagenicaulis* **Exposure:** part shade to sun **Soil:** any **Water needs:** medium **Salt tolerance:** slight **Indoors:** good with intense light and adequate space **Seed germination:** fairly easy but can take as long as two years

Spindle palm should be used as a specimen or accent tree where the swollen trunk and arching fronds can be seen. It is slightly prone to lethal yellowing.

*Hyophorbe lagenicaulis*, bottle base of trunk.
Paul Craft

*Hyophorbe verschaffeltii*, in Florida.

## Hyphaene coriacea
### Doum palm

**Distribution:** tropical eastern Africa and western Madagascar **Growth habit:** sparsely clustering **Height & width:** 30–40 ft. (9–12 m) tall and wide **Trunk(s):** 20–30 ft. (6–9 m) tall, 8–10 in. (20–25 cm) thick, upper parts covered in crisscrossing Y-shaped leaf bases, older parts dark gray with closely set rings or ridges **Crownshaft:** none **Leaves:** palmate, 3–5 ft. (90–150 cm) wide but folding and arching, with deeply cut grayish green to silvery green segments, on stalks 3–5 ft. (90–150 cm) long and armed with heavy spines **Flower clusters:** 2–3 ft. (60–90 cm) long, with a few dark branches bearing white unisexual flowers **Fruit:** pear-shaped, 3 in. (8 cm) long, deep orange to reddish brown when ripe **Growth rate:** slow **Climate:** 9b through 11 **Exposure:** sun **Soil:** any including alkaline media **Water needs:** low, but grows faster with regular irrigation **Salt tolerance:** medium **Indoors:** not good **Seed germination:** easy; within three months; needs a container at least 18 in. (45 cm) deep

*Hyphaene coriacea*, stem bases and suckers, in Florida.

*Hyophorbe verschaffeltii*, detail, in Florida.

*Hyphaene coriacea*, in Florida.

*Hyphaene thebaica*, in Florida.

The large leathery fruits can take one to two years to ripen on the tree. They have fibrous flesh that is edible though not delicious.

## Hyphaene thebaica
### Gingerbread palm, doum palm
**Distribution:** oases and coastal areas of northern and northeastern Africa **Growth habit:** clustering and branching **Height & width:** 40–50 ft. (12–15 m) tall and wide **Trunk(s):** 40–50 ft. (12–15 m) tall, 12–18 in. (30–45 cm) thick, branching naturally into a succession of two-forked divisions; very old specimens almost always have only one trunk that is as much as 3 ft. (90 cm) thick, the massiveness of the many leaf crowns having pushed over the subsidiary trunks **Crownshaft:** none **Leaves:** palmate, 3–5 ft. (90–150 cm) wide but folding and arching, with deeply cut green segments, on stalks 3–5 ft. (90–150 cm) long and armed with heavy spines **Flower clusters:** 2–3 ft. (60–90 cm) long, with a few dark branches bearing white unisexual flowers **Fruit:** similar to those of *Hyphaene coriacea* but never red; edible **Growth rate:** slow **Climate:** 10 and 11 **Exposure:** sun **Soil:** any **Water needs:** low, but grows faster with regular irrigation **Salt tolerance:** medium to high **Indoors:** not good **Seed germination:** easy; within three months; needs a container at least 18 in. (45 cm) deep

Because of the dichotomous trunk branching, gingerbread palm is exceptionally picturesque and appealing at all ages. It is a fabled species with a long record of cultivation and use in ancient Egypt.

*Hyphaene thebaica*, fruit, in Australia. Paul Craft

*Johannesteijsmannia altifrons*, in Costa Rica. Paul Craft

## Johannesteijsmannia altifrons
### Joey palm, diamond joey palm
**Distribution:** rain forests of Malaysia, Thailand, and Borneo from 1000 to 3000 ft. (300–900 m) elevation **Growth habit:** solitary **Height & width:** 12–20 ft. (4–6 m) tall, 15–25 ft. (4.5–7.5 m) wide **Trunk(s):** solitary but underground **Crownshaft:** none **Leaves:** palmate, elongated diamond-shaped, 6–12 ft. (1.8–4 m) long, 6 ft. (1.8 m) wide, unsegmented but deeply pleated, light to deep green above, much lighter beneath, on stalks 6–10 ft. (1.8–3 m) long that have fine spines **Flower clusters:** 2–3 ft. (60–90 cm) long with whitish bisexual flowers **Fruit:** round, 2 in. (5 cm) wide, corky and light brown **Growth rate:** medium **Climate:** 10b and 11, marginal in 10a **Exposure:** part shade **Soil:** deep, humus laden, and slightly acidic **Water needs:** high, with constantly high humidity **Salt tolerance:** none **Indoors:** good with adequate space, light, and moisture **Seed germination:** easy; within two months; needs a container at least 6 in. (15 cm) deep

*Johannesteijsmannia magnifica*, leaf underside.
Paul Craft

*Jubaea chilensis*, in California. Barry Osborne

This incredibly beautiful species is almost maniacally sought after by collectors. It is still rare and always expensive. Joey palm is difficult to maintain in areas with alkaline soil, and drying winds can be devastating to the leaves.

## *Johannesteijsmannia magnifica*
### Blue joey palm
**Distribution:** low mountainous rain forest of peninsular Malaysia **Growth habit:** solitary **Height & width:** 12–20 ft. (4–6 m) tall, 15–25 ft. (4.5–7.5 m) wide **Trunk(s):** solitary but underground **Crownshaft:** none **Leaves:** palmate, elongated diamond-shaped, 6–12 ft. (1.8–4 m) long, 6 ft. (1.8 m) wide, unsegmented but deeply pleated, light to deep green above, covered beneath in a blue to white felt, on stalks 6–10 ft.

(1.8–3 m) long that have fine spines **Flower clusters:** 2–3 ft. (60–90 cm) long with whitish bisexual flowers **Fruit:** round, 2 in. (5 cm) wide, corky and light brown **Growth rate:** medium **Climate:** 10b and 11, marginal in 10a **Exposure:** part shade **Soil:** deep, humus laden, and slightly acidic **Water needs:** high, with constantly high humidity **Salt tolerance:** none **Indoors:** good with adequate space, light, and moisture **Seed germination:** easy; within two months; needs a container at least 6 in. (15 cm) deep

The blue joey palm is usually considered even more beautiful than the diamond joey. It is quite rare, critically endangered in habitat and, if it can be found, is quite expensive. Like the diamond joey, its leaves are damaged by dry winds and the plant is difficult to grow in alkaline soil.

*Jubaea chilensis*, leaf crown, in California. Richard Travis

## *Jubaea chilensis*
### Chilean wine palm

**Distribution:** foothills of the Andes in central Chile **Growth habit:** solitary **Height & width:** 70–100 ft. (21–30 m) tall, 25 ft. (7.5 m) wide **Trunk(s):** 70–80 ft. (21–24 m) tall, 3–6 ft. (90–180 cm) thick, light to dark gray with closely set diamond-shaped and knobby rings, sometimes with a slight bulge near the middle **Crownshaft:** none **Leaves:** pinnate, 8–12 ft. (2.4–4 m) long, with leaflets 2 ft. (60 cm) long that are deep grayish green above, lighter green beneath, on stalks 1 ft. (30 cm) long **Flower clusters:** 4–6 ft. (1.2–1.8 m) long, with branches growing from large, woody bracts and bearing purplish unisexual flowers of both sexes **Fruit:** round, 1 in. (2.5 cm) wide, yellow to deep orange when ripe, seeds are edible **Growth rate:** slow **Climate:** 9 through 11 in humid climes, 8 through 11 in dry climes **Exposure:** sun **Soil:** any **Water needs:** low to medium, but grows faster with regular irrigation **Salt tolerance:** slight **Indoors:** not very good **Seed germination:** easy but may take a year

This palm is one of the few that looks good in straight rows lining a drive or large avenue. It is architectural looking and yet among the most magnificent subjects for a canopy-scape. The plant can take 10 to 20 years to form any stem.

## *Jubaeopsis caffra*
### Pondoland palm

**Distribution:** coastal areas of northeastern South Africa **Growth habit:** sparsely clustering **Height & width:** 20–30 ft. (6–9 m) tall and wide **Trunk(s):** 10–20 ft. (3–6 m) tall, 1–2 ft. (30–60 cm) thick, usually covered in large, tough, widely triangular gray leaf bases **Crownshaft:** none **Leaves:** pinnate, 12–15 ft. (4–4.5 m) long, erect and only slightly arching, usually twisted in the outer half, with narrow, widely spaced, deep to grayish green leaflets that are 3–4 ft. (90–120 cm) long, on yellow to orange stalks 3–4 ft. (90–

*Jubaeopsis caffra*, in California. Barry Osborne

*Jubaeopsis caffra*, trunks, in California. Paul Craft

120 cm) long **Flower clusters:** 3–4 ft. (90–120 cm) long with whitish unisexual flowers of both sexes **Fruit:** round, 1 in. (2.5 cm) wide, yellow when ripe **Growth rate:** slow **Climate:** 10 and 11 **Exposure:** sun **Soil:** any but appreciates humus **Water needs:** medium, but needs regular irrigation for best appearance **Salt tolerance:** little **Indoors:** not very good **Seed germination:** easy but may take a year

Pondoland palm is a beautiful clumper even when young because of the great arching leaves. It gives a wonderful contrast when incorporated into other vegetation and, especially when older, is even beautiful as a specimen surrounded by space.

## Kentiopsis oliviformis

**Distribution:** moist rocky slopes in central New Caledonia **Growth habit:** solitary **Height & width:** 60–80 ft. (18–24 m) tall, 10–20 ft. (3–6 m) wide **Trunk(s):** 50–70 ft. (15–21 m) tall, 1 ft. (30 cm) thick, dark green in all but oldest parts, with widely spaced wide white rings **Crownshaft:** 3 ft. (90 cm) tall, slightly thicker than the trunk, purple to brownish green **Leaves:** pinnate, 10–12 ft. (3–4 m) long, erect to spreading, divided into many closely spaced, dark green leaflets that are 2–3 ft. (60–90 cm) long, on short stalks **Flower clusters:** 2–3 ft. (60–90 cm) wide reddish or purplish sprays of waxy, white unisexual flowers of both sexes

*Kentiopsis oliviformis*, in Florida.

**Fruit:** bullet-shaped, ½ in. (12 mm) long, red when ripe **Growth rate:** medium when given copious supplies of water, slow in drier conditions **Climate:** 10b and 11, marginal in warm parts of 10a **Exposure:** part shade when young, sun when older **Soil:** any but appreciate humus; thrives on alkaline media **Water needs:** high **Salt tolerance:** none **Indoors:** good with bright light and adequate air circulation **Seed germination:** easy in a warm, moist medium; within four months

This palm is of exceptional beauty, both as a juvenile and as a mature specimen. It is majestic enough to be an isolated specimen but looks best in groups of three or more individuals of varying heights and is one of the most beautiful canopy-scapes.

## *Kerriodoxa elegans*
### White elephant palm

**Distribution:** low mountainous rain forest of peninsular Thailand **Growth habit:** solitary **Height & width:** 6–10 ft. (1.8–3 m) tall, 15–20 ft. (4.5–6 m) wide **Trunk(s):** 6–12 ft. (1.8–4 m) tall, 6–8 in. (15–20 cm) thick, upper parts covered in fiber and narrowly triangular leaf bases, lower parts gray to tan with closely set rings or grooves **Crownshaft:** none **Leaves:** palmate, circular, 6–8 ft. (1.8–2.4 m) wide, with segments divided halfway to their depth, grassy to deep emerald green above, chalky white beneath, on black stalks 3 ft. (90 cm) long **Flower clusters:** 18-in. (45-cm) wide sprays of yellow flowers on male trees, 3-ft. (90-cm) wide sprays of yellow flowers on females **Fruit:** round, 2 in. (5 cm)

*Kerriodoxa elegans*, in Florida.

wide, yellow to orange when ripe **Growth rate:** slow **Climate:** 10 and 11, marginal in warm parts of 9b **Exposure:** part shade **Soil:** humus laden **Water needs:** high, with high humidity **Salt tolerance:** none **Indoors:** good **Seed germination:** easy in a warm, moist medium; within one month; needs a container at least 8 in. (20 cm) deep

The great, spreading leaves are astonishingly handsome and spectacular, especially in young plants with little trunk. This species is perfect for a patio or courtyard. Planted in groups of three or more individuals of varying heights, it creates a tableau of near rapturous beauty and, if one has a hillside, nothing could be more splendid than these wonderful leaves seen from above or below.

## *Laccospadix australasica*
### Atherton palm, Queensland kentia

**Distribution:** low mountainous rain forest of northeastern Queensland, Australia **Growth habit:** sparsely clustering but also solitary **Height & width:** clustering types 15–20 ft. (4.5–6 m) tall, 15 ft. (4.5 m) wide; solitaries 25–35 ft. (7.5–10.5 m) tall, 12 ft. (4 m) wide **Trunk(s):** 10 ft. (3 m) tall on clustering types, 25 ft. (7.5 m) tall on solitaries, 4–5 in. (10–13 cm) thick, upper parts deep green, lower parts brown, covered with closely set rings or ridges **Crownshaft:** none **Leaves:** pinnate, 6 ft. (1.8 m) long, erect, unarching, V-shaped in cross section, deep green, often with reddish new growth, on stalks 3 ft. (90 cm) long **Flower clusters:** pendent spikes with white unisexual flowers of both sexes **Fruit:** oblong, ½ in. (12 mm) long, red when ripe **Growth rate:** slow to medium **Climate:** 10 and 11 in cool but frost-free Mediterranean climes **Exposure:** part shade **Soil:** humus laden and slightly acidic **Water needs:** high **Salt tolerance:** none **Indoors:** very good **Seed germination:** easy; within two months

Atherton palm is an elegant and graceful small tree. The clustering forms are a veritable symphony of lovely leaf forms among other vegetation, and the solitary-trunked form is scintillating

*Laccospadix australasica*, in California. Barry Osborne

when surrounded by space and a short groundcover, all under canopy.

## *Latania loddigesii*
### Blue latan palm

**Distribution:** savannas of the Mascarene Islands **Growth habit:** solitary **Height & width:** 50 ft. (15 m) tall, 12 ft. (4 m) wide **Trunk(s):** 20–35 ft. (6–10.5 m) tall, 10 in. (25 cm) thick, deep gray with closely set rings or ridges **Crownshaft:** none **Leaves:** palmate, 6–8 ft. (1.8–2.4 m) wide but folded, with stiff, bluish gray to silvery blue segments extending halfway to the 4- to 6- ft.

*Latania loddigesii*, in Florida.

*Latania lontaroides*, male flowers, in Florida.

## *Latania lontaroides*
### Red latan palm

**Distribution:** savannas of the Mascarene Islands **Growth habit:** solitary **Height & width:** 50 ft. (15 m) tall, 12 ft. (4 m) wide **Trunk(s):** 20–35 ft. (6–10.5 m) tall, 10 in. (25 cm) thick, deep gray with closely set rings or ridges **Crownshaft:** none **Leaves:** palmate, 6–8 ft. (1.8–2.4 m) wide, folded, not as stiff as those of *Latania loddigesii*, with leaf stalks and blades of younger trees having much red color, while leaves of older plants are deep green above and grayish green beneath, leaf crown round **Flower clusters:** 3- to 4-ft. (90- to 120-cm) long branches on female trees **Fruit:** ovoid, 3 in. (8 cm) long, brown **Growth rate:** medium to slow **Climate:** 10b and 11, marginal in 10a **Exposure:** sun **Soil:** any including alkaline media **Water needs:** medium **Salt tolerance:** slight **Indoors:** only with intense light and perfect air circulation **Seed germination:** within a year; needs a container at least 6 in. (15 cm) deep

Although gorgeous, the red latan palm is not as easy to find as the blue latan. Like that species, however, it is slightly prone to lethal yellowing.

(1.2- to 1.8-long) stalk, outer margins tinged with red in young plants, leaf crown round **Flower clusters:** 3- to 4-ft. (90- to 120-cm) long branches on female trees **Fruit:** ovoid, 3 in. (8 cm) long, brown **Growth rate:** medium to slow **Climate:** 10b and 11, marginal in 10a **Exposure:** sun **Soil:** any including alkaline media **Water needs:** medium **Salt tolerance:** slight **Indoors:** only with intense light and perfect air circulation **Seed germination:** within a year; needs a container at least 6 in. (15 cm) deep

Blue latan palm is spectacular because of its coloring and height and width. This dark beauty looks superb in almost any site. It also makes a thrilling canopy-scape. Unfortunately, it is slightly prone to lethal yellowing.

*Latania lontaroides*, in Florida.

## Latania verschaffeltii
### Yellow latan palm

**Distribution:** savannas of the Mascarene Islands
**Growth habit:** solitary **Height & width:** 50 ft.
(15 m) tall, 12 ft. (4 m) wide **Trunk(s):** 20–35 ft.
(6–10.5 m) tall, 10 in. (25 cm) thick, deep gray
with closely set rings or ridges **Crownshaft:**
none **Leaves:** palmate, 6–8 ft. (1.8–2.4 m) wide,
folded, less stiff than those of *Latania loddige-*
*sii*, yellow-green on both surfaces, leaf stalks of
younger trees are entirely yellow with white cot-
tonlike fibers **Flower clusters:** 3- to 4-ft. (90- to
120-cm) long branches on female trees **Fruit:**
ovoid, 3 in. (8 cm) long, brown **Growth rate:**
medium to slow **Climate:** 10b and 11, marginal
in 10a **Exposure:** sun **Soil:** any including alkaline media **Water needs:** medium **Salt toler-**
**ance:** slight **Indoors:** only with intense light
and perfect air circulation **Seed germination:**
within a year; needs a container at least 6 in.
(15 cm) deep

*Latania verschaffeltii*, in Florida.

Yellow latan palm is gorgeous but not nearly as easy to find as the blue latan palm. Like its relatives, it is slightly prone to lethal yellowing.

*Latania verschaffeltii*, trunk, in Florida.

## Licuala cordata

**Distribution:** low mountainous rain forest of Sarawak **Growth habit:** solitary **Height & width:** 4 ft. (1.2 m) tall, 5–6 ft. (1.5–1.8 m) wide **Trunk(s):** less than 1 ft. (30 cm) tall and usually not apparent **Crownshaft:** none **Leaves:** palmate, circular with a narrow lobe at the base, 1½–2 ft. (45–60 cm) wide, lustrous emerald green, distinctly corrugated, usually unsegmented but some individuals have six to eight wedge-shaped segments **Flower clusters:** short sprays of white bisexual flowers **Fruit:** round, small, red **Growth rate:** slow **Climate:** 10b and 11 **Exposure:** shade to part shade **Soil:** humus laden **Water needs:** medium to high **Salt tolerance:** none **Indoors:** excellent **Seed germination:** erratic and usually slow; as long as a year or more

This species can be somewhat hard to find. Plants with segmented leaves are rarer than those with entire leaves but far less desirable in the landscape.

## Licuala grandis
### Ruffled fan palm

**Distribution:** rain forest of the Solomon Islands and Vanuatu **Growth habit:** solitary **Height & width:** 12–20 ft. (4–6 m) tall, 8 ft. (2.4 m) wide **Trunk(s):** 8–12 ft. (2.4–4 m) tall, 3 in. (8 cm) thick, upper parts with dense fiber and narrow

*Licuala cordata*, segmented leaf form, in Australia. Paul Craft

*Licuala cordata*, unsegmented leaf form, in Australia. Paul Craft

*Licuala grandis*, in Florida.

leaf bases, lower parts gray with closely set rings or grooves **Crownshaft:** none **Leaves:** palmate, semicircular to broadly wedge- or diamond-shaped, 3 ft. (90 cm) wide, unsegmented, corrugated, deep green on 3-ft. (90-cm) long stalks that have small spines at their base **Flower clusters:** short yellowish sprays of bisexual flowers **Fruit:** round, ½ in. (12 mm) wide, red, in pendent clusters **Growth rate:** medium to slow **Climate:** 10b and 11, marginal in 10a **Exposure:** part shade when young, adaptable to sun when older except in hot climates **Soil:** humus laden **Water needs:** high, with high humidity **Salt tolerance:** none **Indoors:** excellent **Seed germination:** erratic and usually slow; as long as a year or more

This small frost-sensitive palm is among the choicest in the world. It has an exquisite elegance matched by few other species. The leaf crowns are stunning when planted in groups of three or more individuals of varying heights and as ac-cents in masses of other vegetation. It is perfect as a patio or courtyard subject where its beauty may be enjoyed up close.

## *Licuala mattanensis 'Mapu'*
### Mapu palm

**Distribution:** lowland rain forest of Sarawak **Growth habit:** solitary **Height & width:** 3 ft. (90 cm) tall, 4–6 ft. (1.2–1.8 m) wide **Trunk(s):** very short or underground **Crownshaft:** none **Leaves:** palmate, semicircular to completely circular, with 12 deeply divided segments covered by beautiful yellow splotches, on unarmed stalks 1½–2 ft. (45–60 cm) long **Flower clusters:** short with whitish bisexual flowers **Fruit:** round, small, reddish brown **Growth rate:** slow **Climate:** 11, marginal in 10b **Exposure:** shade to part shade **Soil:** humus laden and definitely acidic **Water needs:** high, with high humidity **Salt tolerance:** none **Indoors:** excellent **Seed germination:** erratic and usually slow; as long as a year or more

*Licuala mattanensis* 'Mapu', in Australia. Paul Craft

This very beautiful cultivated variety is much sought after. Compared to the species, 'Mapu' is less tender and less finicky about soil type.

## Licuala orbicularis

**Distribution:** lowland rain forest of Sarawak **Growth habit:** solitary **Height & width:** 6–8 ft. (1.8–2.4 m) tall, 12–15 ft. (4–4.5 m) wide **Trunk(s):** very short or underground **Crownshaft:** none **Leaves:** palmate, shaped like a Victorian fan, 3–5 ft. (90–150 cm) wide, unsegmented, corrugated, deep glossy green above and lighter green beneath, on thin stalks 6 ft. (1.8 m) long **Flower clusters:** arching sprays 3 ft. (90 cm) long bearing whitish bisexual flowers **Fruit:** round, ½ in. (12 mm) wide, bright red **Growth rate:** slow **Climate:** 10b and 11 **Exposure:** part shade **Soil:** humus laden **Water needs:** high **Salt tolerance:** none **Indoors:** perfect **Seed germination:** erratic and usually slow; as long as a year or more

This palm is an astonishingly beautiful accent plant for shady areas. Its great, shiny, rounded, and corrugated blades add an almost unique elegance and charm to tropical sites otherwise difficult to landscape.

## Licuala peltata

**Distribution:** northeastern India to peninsular Malaysia in low to mountainous rain forests **Growth habit:** solitary **Height & width:** 20–30 ft. (6–9 m) tall, 15–20 ft. (4.5–6 m) wide **Trunk(s):** 10–20 ft. (3–6 m) tall, 3–4 in. (8–10 cm) thick, upper parts covered with dense fibers **Crownshaft:** none **Leaves:** palmate, 6 ft. (1.8 m) wide, corrugated, divided into 15 to 25 wedge-shaped, glossy deep green segments, on armed stalks 8–12 ft. (2.4–4 m) long **Flower clusters:** erect, 10–12 ft. (3–4 m) long, bearing yellowish bisexual flowers **Fruit:** round, ½ in. (12 mm) wide, dark red **Growth rate:** medium **Climate:** 10 and 11, marginal in warm parts of 9b **Exposure:** part

*Licuala orbicularis*, in Australia. Paul Craft

shade, especially when young, adaptable to full sun when older except in hot climates **Soil:** any including alkaline media; benefits from a mulch **Water needs:** medium to high **Salt tolerance:** none **Indoors:** good with enough light, humidity, and space **Seed germination:** erratic and usually slow; as long as a year or more

This palm is so attractive that it is hard to misplace in the garden if given enough space; it should not be crowded into tight spaces with other vegetation. It should be planted in a wind-protected site as its leaf blades are relatively thin and become easily tattered, but, even then, it is unusually beautiful.

*Licuala peltata*, in Australia. Paul Craft

*Licuala peltata* var. *sumawongii*, in Florida.

Var. *sumawongii* (synonym *Licuala elegans*) differs from var. *peltata* in having unsegmented leaves which are completely circular in outline.

## Licuala ramsayi

**Distribution:** swampy to well-drained lowland rain forest of northeastern Queensland, Australia **Growth habit:** solitary **Height & width:** 30–50 ft. (9–15 m) tall, 18 ft. (5.4 m) wide **Trunk(s):** 20–35 ft. (6–10.5 m) tall, 8 in. (20 cm) thick, light gray to nearly white **Crownshaft:** none **Leaves:** palmate, circular, 5–6 ft. (1.5–1.8 m) wide, with 10 to 12 corrugated, deep green, wedge-shaped segments divided to their depth, on stalks 6 ft. (1.8 m) long **Flower clusters:** erect, 10–12 ft. (3–4 m) long, bearing whitish bisexual flowers **Fruit:** round, 1 in. (2.5 cm) wide, bright red **Growth rate:** medium **Climate:** 10b and 11 **Exposure:** part shade; can adapt to full sun when older **Soil:** humus laden **Water needs:** high **Salt tolerance:**

*Licuala ramsayi*, roots of a mature tree, in Australia. Paul Craft

*Licuala ramsayi*, leaf outline, in Australia. Chuck Hubbuch

*Licuala ramsayi*, in Australia. Paul Craft

none **Indoors:** good with sufficient space, light, and moisture **Seed germination:** erratic and usually slow; as long as a year or more

The incredibly beautiful leaves are shaped like pinwheels. Mature individuals make perhaps the finest of all canopy-scapes.

## Licuala spinosa
### Mangrove fan palm, spiny licuala

**Distribution:** coastal plains of the Nicobar Islands to western Indonesia and the Philippine Islands **Growth habit:** densely clustering **Height & width:** 20 ft. (6 m) tall, 15–20 ft. (4.5–6 m) wide **Trunk(s):** 12–15 ft. (4–4.5 m) tall, 3 in. (8 cm) thick, upper parts covered in dense fibers, lower parts almost smooth and nearly white **Crownshaft:** none **Leaves:** palmate, circular, 2–3 ft. (60–90 cm) wide, divided into 10 to 15 wedge-shaped, corrugated, light to deep green segments with squared, jagged ends, on thin stalks 3–4 ft. (90–120 cm) long with curved spines **Flower clusters:** erect spikes 4–8 ft. (1.2–2.4 m) long bearing yellowish bisexual flowers **Fruit:** round, ¼ in. (6 mm) wide, bright red **Growth rate:** medium to fast **Climate:** 10 and 11, marginal in warm parts of 9b **Exposure:** part shade to full sun **Soil:** any but best with some humus **Water needs:** high **Salt tolerance:** good **Indoors:** good with intense light and humidity **Seed germination:** erratic and usually slow; as long as a year or more

A splendid (but very spiny) hedge subject, mangrove fan palm is also perfect as a large accent among other vegetation, in which case it looks better if a few of the trunks (especially those of the same height) are judiciously pruned out so that the wonderful silhouette of the leaves is more readily apparent.

*Licuala spinosa*, in Panama. Paul Craft

*Licuala spinosa*, leaf detail, in Florida.

*Livistona australis*, in California. Richard Travis

## Livistona australis
## Australian fan palm, Australian cabbage palm

**Distribution:** savannas, hilly forests, and swamps along eastern coastal Australia from central Queensland to Victoria **Growth habit:** solitary **Height & width:** 45–60 ft. (13.5–18 m) tall, 15 ft. (4.5 m) wide **Trunk(s):** 40–60 ft. (12–18 m) tall, 1 ft. (30 cm) thick, light to dark gray or brown with closely spaced rings or grooves **Crownshaft:** none **Leaves:** palmate, semicircular to nearly circular, 5 ft. (1.5 m) wide, divided into deep, dark green to grayish green segments that are pendent for at least half their length, on armed stalks 6 ft. (1.8 m) long **Flower clusters:** 4 ft. (1.2 m) long with white bisexual flowers **Fruit:** round, ½ in. (12 mm) wide, black when ripe **Growth rate:** medium to fast **Climate:** 9 through 11, marginal in warm parts of 8a **Exposure:** sun to part shade **Soil:** adaptable but best with humus **Water needs:** medium, but grows faster and looks better with regular irrigation **Salt tolerance:** slight **Indoors:** only with space and intense light **Seed germination:** easy; within three months; needs a container at least 6 in. (15 cm) deep

Because of its beautiful and graceful pendent leaf segments, this palm is perfect as a canopyscape, especially in groups of individuals of different heights.

## Livistona chinensis
## Chinese fan palm

**Distribution:** open woods of the southern Japanese islands, Taiwan, and southern China **Growth habit:** solitary **Height & width:** 40–50 ft. (12–15 m) tall, 15–18 ft. (4.5–5.4 m) wide **Trunk(s):** 30–40 ft. (9–12 m) tall, 1 ft. (30 cm) thick, brown to reddish brown when young, gray when old with closely set rings or grooves **Crownshaft:** none **Leaves:** palmate, circular, 6 ft. (1.8 m) wide, deeply divided into grassy to

Livistona chinensis, in Florida.

*Livistona chinensis*, leaf crown, in the Dominican Republic. Paul Craft

*Livistona chinensis*, in Texas.

deep green segments that are flat in young trees but pendent for half their length in older trees **Flower clusters:** 6 ft. (1.8 m) long and arching, bearing whitish bisexual flowers **Fruit:** round to ovoid, 1 in. (2.5 cm) wide, greenish blue to pinkish gray when ripe **Growth rate:** medium **Climate:** 9 through 11, marginal in 8b **Exposure:** part shade to full sun in all but the hottest climes **Soil:** best with humus but adaptable **Water needs:** medium **Salt tolerance:** little **Indoors:** good with adequate space and intense light **Seed germination:** easy; within three months; needs a container at least 6 in. (15 cm) deep

The Chinese fan palm has the same landscape uses as the Australian fan palm but is more choice as a young plant because of its wide, nearly circular leaves, especially when grown in partial shade. It is great for smaller yards and is only slightly prone to lethal yellowing.

## Livistona decora
### Ribbon fan palm

**Synonym:** *Livistona decipiens* **Distribution:** coastal forests and swamps of Queensland, Australia **Growth habit:** solitary **Height & width:** 50–70 ft. (15–21 m) tall, 15 ft. (4.5 m) wide **Trunk(s):** 40–50 ft. (12–15 m) tall, 10 in. (25 cm) thick, light brown with closely set rings or grooves **Crownshaft:** none **Leaves:** palmate, 9 ft. (2.7 m) wide but folded and curved along the midrib, with very deep, thin, deep green to grayish green segments that are completely pendent for most of their length **Flower clusters:** 8 ft. (2.4 m) long, arching out of the crown, bearing yellow bisexual flowers **Fruit:** round, ½ in. (12 mm) wide, black when ripe **Growth rate:** medium to fast **Climate:** 9 through 11, marginal in 8b **Exposure:** sun **Soil:** any **Water needs:** medium, but grows faster with regular irrigation **Salt tolerance:** slight **Indoors:** not very good **Seed germination:** easy; within three months; needs a container at least 6 in. (15 cm) deep

Because of the weeping curtain effect of the leaf segments, the leaf crown of this palm provides one of the most beautiful silhouettes in nature and its canopy-scape is almost spellbinding.

*Livistona decora*, in Florida.

## Livistona drudei

**Distribution:** coastal plains of northeastern Queensland, Australia **Growth habit:** solitary **Height & width:** 50–70 ft. (15–21 m) tall, 15–20 ft. (4.5–6 m) wide **Trunk(s):** 50–80 ft. (15–24 m) tall, 1 ft. (30 cm) thick, light gray to almost white, without fibers or leaf bases when older, usually with both when young **Crownshaft:** none **Leaves:** palmate, semicircular to diamond-shaped, with narrow, deep green to grayish green segments that extend halfway to the stalk and are mostly pendent **Flower clusters:** 5–7 ft. (1.5–2.1 m) long with yellowish white bisexual flowers **Fruit:** round, ½ in. (12 mm) wide, pur-

*Livistona drudei*, in Florida.

*Livistona mariae*, in Florida. Paul Craft

plish black when ripe **Growth rate:** medium to fast **Climate:** 10 and 11, marginal in warm parts of 9b **Exposure:** sun **Soil:** any including alkaline media **Water needs:** medium, but grows faster with regular irrigation **Salt tolerance:** slight **Indoors:** not good **Seed germination:** easy; within three months; needs a container at least 6 in. (15 cm) deep

With its open, circular leaf crown and long leaf stalks, this species has a thrilling, airy silhouette.

## *Livistona mariae*
### Central Australian fan palm

**Distribution:** desert canyons in northern and central Australia **Growth habit:** solitary **Height & width:** 70–90 ft. (21–27 m) tall, 15 ft. (4.5 m) wide **Trunk(s):** 70–80 ft. (21–24 m) tall, 1 ft. (30 cm) thick, dark to light gray and almost smooth when old, with dense fibers and triangular leaf bases when young **Crownshaft:** none

**Leaves:** palmate, 6–8 ft. (1.8–2.4 m) wide but folded along the midrib, divided into deep, grayish green segments that are pendent for most of their length, on reddish brown stalks 6–8 ft. (1.8–2.4 m) long and armed with large spines **Flower clusters:** 6–8 ft. (1.8–2.4 m) long, erect, bearing yellow bisexual flowers **Fruit:** round, ½ in. (12 mm) wide, black when ripe **Growth rate:** quite fast **Climate:** 10 and 11, dry parts of 9b **Exposure:** sun **Soil:** any including alkaline media **Water needs:** drought tolerant, but grows much faster with regular irrigation **Salt tolerance:** medium **Indoors:** not good **Seed germination:** easy; within three months; needs a container at least 6 in. (15 cm) deep

Similar in form but more robust than the ribbon fan palm, the central Australian fan palm has a canopy-scape that is possibly even more thrilling. Juvenile plants are reddish or maroon in color.

*Livistona nitida*

*Livistona nitida*, detail, in Florida.

## *Livistona nitida*
### Carnarvon Gorge fan palm
Synonym: *Livistona* 'Carnarvon Gorge' **Distribution:** along creeks and rivers of southeastern Queensland, Australia **Growth habit:** solitary **Height & width:** 70–100 ft. (21–30 m) tall, 20 ft. (6 m) wide **Trunk(s):** 70–90 ft. (21–27 m) tall, 1 ft. (30 cm) thick, light gray to reddish brown with closely set rings or grooves **Crownshaft:** none **Leaves:** palmate, 6 ft. (1.8 m) wide, deeply divided into pendent, deep glossy green to grayish green segments, on stalks that are 6–8 ft. (1.8–2.4 m) long and armed with tiny spines **Flower clusters:** 4–5 ft. (1.2–1.5 m) long, erect, bearing yellow bisexual flowers **Fruit:** round, ½ in. (12 mm) wide, glossy black when ripe **Growth rate:** medium to fast **Climate:** 8b through 11, marginal in warm, dry parts of 8a **Exposure:** sun **Soil:** any **Water needs:** medium **Salt tolerance:** slight **Indoors:** not good **Seed germination:** easy; within three months; needs a container at least 6 in. (15 cm) deep

This beautiful species is similar in most respects to *Livistona australis* but more robust, even hardier to cold and faster growing.

## *Livistona rotundifolia*
### Footstool palm, round-leaf fan palm
**Distribution:** low mountainous rain forests of Malaysia to the Philippine Islands **Growth habit:** solitary **Height & width:** 60–70 ft. (18–21 m) tall, 15–30 ft. (4.5–9 m) wide **Trunk(s):** 60–70 ft. (18–21 m) tall, 1 ft. (30 cm) thick, light gray with widely spaced, thick dark rings **Crownshaft:** none **Leaves:** palmate, completely circular in young trees, less so in older trees, 5–6 ft. (1.5–1.8 m) wide, deep green, leaf crown extended in younger trees but smaller and round in old ones **Flower clusters:** 8 ft. (2.4 m) long, bearing yellow bisexual flowers **Fruit:** round, 1 in. (2.5 cm)

*Livistona rotundifolia*, in the Dominican Republic. Paul Craft

*Livistona rotundifolia*, trunk, in Florida.

wide, bright red turning glossy black when ripe **Growth rate:** medium to fast **Climate:** 10b and 11, marginal in 10a **Exposure:** part shade when young, full sun when older **Soil:** any including alkaline media **Water needs:** high **Salt tolerance:** none **Indoors:** only as a juvenile **Seed germination:** easy; within three months; needs a container at least 6 in. (15 cm) deep

Because young plants have larger, less deeply segmented leaves than do adults, they are stunningly attractive up close, looking more like disks than fan leaves, and are choice for intimate areas. The leaf crown of older trees is open and exquisitely graceful, and is among the finest canopy-scapes. When planted in groups of three or more individuals of varying heights, this palm is even more attractive. It is slightly prone to lethal yellowing.

### *Livistona saribus*
Taraw palm
**Distribution:** coastal swamps and rain forest clearings of southeastern China, Southeast Asia, and the Philippine Islands **Growth habit:** solitary **Height & width:** 50–60 ft. (15–18 m) tall, 15

*Livistona saribus*, fibrous trunk and spiny leaf stalks, in Florida.

*Livistona saribus*, juvenile plants in shade. Paul Craft

ft. (4.5 m) wide **Trunk(s):** 40–50 ft. (12–15 m) tall, 1 ft. (30 cm) thick, gray to reddish brown **Crownshaft:** none **Leaves:** palmate, circular, 4 ft. (1.2 m) wide, semisegmented into a few broad divisions on young plants, divided into slightly pendent segments halfway to the stalk on older plants, grassy to deep green, on stalks 5–6 ft. (1.5–1.8 m) long, sometimes red, with vicious but beautiful backward-pointing spines **Flower clusters:** 5 ft. (1.5 m) long and mostly erect, bearing yellow bisexual flowers **Fruit:** round, 1 in. (2.5 cm) wide, shiny blue or purple **Growth rate:** medium **Climate:** 10 and 11, marginal in warm parts of 9b **Exposure:** part shade when young, full sun when older **Soil:** any including alkaline media **Water needs:** high **Salt tolerance:** medium **Indoors:** only as a juvenile **Seed germination:** easy; within three months; needs a container at least 6 in. (15 cm) deep

Juvenile plants are much more interesting than adult plants because of the larger, less-segmented flat leaves and the beautiful thorns on the leaf stalk.

## *Lytocaryum weddellianum*
## Miniature coconut palm

**Synonym:** *Microcoelum weddellianum* **Distribution:** low mountainous rain forest of coastal southern Brazil **Growth habit:** solitary **Height & width:** 10–15 ft. (3–4.5 m) tall, 6–8 ft. (1.8–2.4 m) wide **Trunk(s):** 6–10 ft. (1.8–3 m) tall, 3–4 in. (8–10 cm) thick, mostly covered in dense, dark brown fibers and narrow tan leaf base stubs **Crownshaft:** none **Leaves:** pinnate, 2–3 ft. (60–90 cm) long, arching, divided into evenly spaced leaflets that are 4–6 in. (10–15 cm) long and dark green above and silvery gray beneath, on stalks 1 ft. (30 m) long **Flower clusters:** 3–4 ft. (90–120 cm) long with pendent branches emerging from narrow woody capsule-like bracts and bearing yellowish unisexual flowers of both sexes **Fruit:** round, ¾ in. (2 cm) wide, turquoise becoming brown and splitting when ripe **Growth rate:** medium to slow **Climate:** 10 and 11, marginal in warmest parts of 9b **Exposure:** part shade **Soil:** humus laden and somewhat acidic **Water needs:** high, with high humidity **Salt tolerance:**

*Lytocaryum weddellianum*, in California. Barry Osborne

none **Indoors:** perfect **Seed germination:** slow; within a year

This remarkably beautiful miniature palm has as many visual affinities with a giant fern as it does with a palm species. It is one of the finest container plants for part shade.

## *Mauritia flexuosa*

**Distribution:** in plains and flatland swamps and along rivers in northern South America east of the Andes **Growth habit:** solitary **Height & width:** 60–80 ft. (18–24 m) tall, 30–45 ft. (9–13.5 m) wide **Trunk(s):** 40–60 ft. (12–18 m) tall, 1–2 ft. (30–60 cm) thick, light gray with widely spaced dark rings **Crownshaft:** none **Leaves:** palmate, circular, 15 ft. (4.5 m) wide, divided into many stiff, dark green, 6-ft. (1.8-m) long leaflets growing at different angles along the curving midrib to give a plumose-pinnate look, leaf crown hemispherical without the dead leaves, spherical with them, on massive stalks that are 20–30 ft. (6–9 m) long and 4 ft. (1.2 m) thick at the base **Flower clusters:** 6-ft. (1.8-m) long horizontal curtains of unisexual flowers **Fruit:** oblong, 3 in. (8 cm) long, covered with overlapping scales,

*Mauritia flexuosa*, in Australia. Paul Craft

*Mauritia flexuosa*, flowers, in Australia. Paul Craft

*Mauritia flexuosa*, silhouette, in Ecuador. Chuck Hubbuch

deep red, in pendent clusters **Growth rate:** fast **Climate:** 11, marginal in 10b **Exposure:** part shade when young, full sun when older **Soil:** humus laden and acidic **Water needs:** high **Salt tolerance:** none **Indoors:** not good **Seed germination:** easy; within two months in a warm, moist medium

The massive size and form of this palm are breathtaking and unbelievably beautiful in any site.

## Metroxylon amicarum
### Caroline ivory-nut palm

**Distribution:** low mountainous rain forest of the Caroline Islands of Micronesia **Growth habit:** solitary **Height & width:** 60–80 ft. (18–24 m) tall, 15–20 ft. (4.5–6 m) wide **Trunk(s):** 45–60 ft. (13.5–18 m) tall, 1–2 ft. (30–60 cm) thick, upper parts covered in massive triangular leaf bases, lower parts light gray with widely spaced dark rings **Crownshaft:** none **Leaves:** pinnate, plumose, 15 ft. (4.5 m) long, dark green, on massive 4-ft. (1.2-m) long stalks that have wavy lines of dark spines on their bases **Flower clusters:** 5–6 ft. (1.5–1.8 m) long, erect, growing out of the leaf bases, bearing unisexual flowers of both sexes **Fruit:** ovoid, 3 in. (8 cm) long, covered in overlapping scales, glossy reddish brown when ripe **Growth rate:** fast once past the juvenile stage **Climate:** 10b and 11 **Exposure:** part shade when young, full sun when older **Soil:** humus laden **Water needs:** high **Salt tolerance:** none **Indoors:** only as a juvenile or in a giant conservatory or atrium **Seed germination:** easy in a warm, moist medium but the very hard seed must be soaked in warm water for a few days; within two months

Caroline ivory-nut palm makes a massive and beautiful conversation piece in the landscape.

*Metroxylon amicarum*, leaf sheaths, in Australia. Paul Craft

*Metroxylon amicarum*, in Australia. Paul Craft

*Metroxylon sagu*, in Australia. Paul Craft

*Metroxylon sagu*, new leaf color, in Australia. Paul Craft

## *Metroxylon sagu*
### Sago palm

**Distribution:** unknown; now naturalized all over the Asian wet tropics **Growth habit:** clustering **Height & width:** 40–60 ft. (12–18 m) tall, 30–40 ft. (9–12 m) wide **Trunk(s):** 20–30 ft. (6–9 m) tall, 1–2 ft. (30–60 cm) thick **Crownshaft:** none **Leaves:** pinnate, 20 ft. (6 m) long, erect but arching, V-shaped in cross section, with stiff, dark green leaflets 4–5 ft. (1.2–1.5 m) long, on 6-ft. (1.8-m) long stalks with massive bases covered with wavy rows of golden spines 3 in. (8 cm) long, leaf crown shaped like a shuttlecock **Flower clusters:** 25 ft. (7.5 m) tall with tiered branches growing from the top of the stem and bearing unisexual flowers of both sexes **Fruit:** round, 2–4 in. (5–10 cm) wide, covered in overlapping scales, brown when ripe **Growth rate:** fast **Climate:** 10b and 11, marginal in 10a **Exposure:** sun **Soil:** rich and deep **Water needs:** very high **Salt tolerance:** slight **Indoors:** only with much space, light, and warmth **Seed germination:** easy in a warm, moist medium; within two months

This is one of the world's most impressive palms. Because of its suckering habit, it can make a great tiered wall of sumptuously beautiful and tropical-looking foliage. New growth is golden, red, or maroon.

## *Nannorrhops ritchiana*
### Mazari palm

**Distribution:** mountainous regions of the Middle East, near springs and seepages **Growth habit:** clustering **Height & width:** 6–20 ft. (1.8–6 m) tall, 8–15 ft. (2.4–4.5 m) wide **Trunk(s):**

*Nannorrhops ritchiana*, in Florida.

*Nannorrhops ritchiana*, inflorescences growing from the top of the trunk, in Florida.

*Nannorrhops ritchiana*, an unusual weeping form, in Florida.

often very short but occasionally to 15 ft. (4.5 m) tall, 8 in. (20 cm) thick, covered in orange-brown fibers and brown leaf bases **Crownshaft:** none **Leaves:** palmate, semicircular to wedge-shaped, 4 ft. (1.2 m) wide, with deep, usually stiff, dark green to bluish silvery segments, on stalks 3 ft. (90 cm) long, usually with spiny margins **Flower clusters:** 6 ft. (1.8 m) long, erect, growing from the top of the trunk, with tiered branches bearing white bisexual flowers **Fruit:** round, ½ in. (12 mm) wide, orange-brown when ripe **Growth rate:** slow **Climate:** 8b through 11 in moist climes, marginal in dry parts of 7 **Exposure:** sun **Soil:** any including alkaline media **Water needs:** low **Salt tolerance:** high **Indoors:** not good **Seed germination:** easy with warmth; within

one month; needs a container at least 6 in. (15 cm) deep

Because of its form, color, and hardiness, the species is valuable as a strong accent along sunny paths and in sunny borders or the cactus and succulent garden. It makes a nice potted specimen for outdoors, but the container must have unimpeded drainage. This palm is slightly prone to lethal yellowing.

## *Nypa fruticans*
### Nipa, mangrove palm

**Distribution:** estuaries, lagoons, and rivers of coastal floodplains from India to the southern Japanese islands and the South Seas Islands **Growth habit:** clustering, creeping **Height & width:** 30–40 ft. (9–12 m) tall, 20 ft. (6 m) wide **Trunk(s):** mostly submerged in mud, 6–10 ft. (1.8–3 m) long, 2 ft. (60 cm) thick, succulent **Crownshaft:** none **Leaves:** pinnate, 20–25 ft.

*Nypa fruticans* at Montgomery Botanical Center, Miami, Florida.

(6–7.5 m) long, erect and barely arching when new, spreading and somewhat arching when older, divided into regularly spaced light to dark green leaflets, each 3 ft. (90 cm) long **Flower clusters**: erect, growing from the leaf bases, bearing a large, round mass of purplish female flowers above yellow male flowers, the whole affair atop a stalk that is 3–5 ft. (90–150 cm) long **Fruit**: round, 3 in. (8 cm) long, shiny brown, in conical masses 1 ft. (30 cm) wide **Growth rate**: fast **Climate**: 10b and 11 **Exposure**: sun **Soil**: any dry medium; does not need salinity to flourish **Water needs**: very high **Salt tolerance**: good **Indoors**: not good **Seed germination**: quick and easy with warmth

This fantastic species has a tropical but wild and primitive demeanor. It creates a true "jungle" aspect like no other species can when planted around ponds or lakes. Fortunate is the tropical gardener who has room to grow it.

*Nypa fruticans*, fruit, in Florida.

*Oncosperma tigillarium*, in Florida.

*Oncosperma tigillarium*, trunk, in Florida.

## Oncosperma tigillarium

**Distribution:** coastal swamps of Southeast Asia and Indonesia **Growth habit:** densely clustering **Height & width:** 80–100 ft. (24–30 m) tall, 25–40 ft. (7.5–12 m) wide **Trunk(s):** 50–80 ft. (15–24 m) tall, 6 in. (15 cm) thick, light brown to light gray with many 2- to 4-in. (5- to 10-cm) long black spines and very widely spaced darker, thin rings **Crownshaft:** 5 ft. (1.5 m) tall, pale green, cylindrical, with short black spines **Leaves:** pinnate, 10 ft. (3 m) long, arching, with pendent, 2-ft. (60-cm) long light to dark green leaflets, on stalks 2 ft. (60 cm) long, both stalks and midribs have short black spines **Flower clusters:** 3 ft. (90 cm) long, pendent, bearing yellow unisexual flowers of both sexes **Fruit:** round, 1 in. (2.5 cm) wide, dark purple when ripe **Growth rate:** medium to fast **Climate:** 10b and 11 **Exposure:** sun **Soil:** any including alkaline media **Water needs:** high **Salt tolerance:** medium **Indoors:** only with much space and light **Seed germination:** easy in a warm, moist medium; within two months

The great height and density of the clumps, as well as the array of different heights of leaf crowns with their beautifully arching leaves and curtains of pendent leaflets, make this palm a veritable symphony, almost a world unto itself, of glorious forms. Some old individuals have one or a few much more dominant stems, which only add to the incredible beauty of the clump.

## Parajubaea cocoides
### Mountain coconut palm, Quito coconut palm

**Distribution:** known only from cultivated trees in central Ecuador and southwestern Colombia at elevations between 7,500 and 10,000 ft. (2250–3000 m) **Growth habit:** solitary **Height & width:** 40–60 ft. (12–18 m) tall, 15 ft. (4.5 m) wide **Trunk(s):** 30–50 ft. (9–15 m) tall, 18 in. (45 cm) thick, covered in dark brown fibers and lighter brown leaf bases when young, mostly smooth and dark gray when older **Crownshaft:** none **Leaves:** pinnate, 10–12 ft. (3–4 m) long, arching, with deep, glossy green 2-ft. (60-cm) long leaflets, midrib twisted so that leaflets at the outer

*Parajubaea cocoides*, in California. Richard Travis

half are vertically oriented, leaf crown normally round **Flower clusters:** sprays 3 ft. (90 cm) long bearing yellow-orange unisexual flowers of both sexes **Fruit:** round, 3 in. (8 cm) wide, dark green to brown when ripe **Growth rate:** slow **Climate:** 9b through 11 in cool but frost-free Mediterranean climes **Exposure:** sun **Soil:** any **Water needs:** low **Salt tolerance:** none **Indoors:** not good **Seed germination:** slow; within two years; the very hard seed should be soaked for a few days

The stunningly attractive and tropical-looking leaf crown resembles that of a coconut palm and makes it is almost impossible to believe that the species is native to an elevated, nontropical habitat.

## *Parajubaea torallyi*
### Bolivian mountain coconut

**Distribution:** semiarid valleys of western Bolivia from elevations of 4500 to 6500 ft. (1350–1950 m) **Growth habit:** solitary **Height & width:** 30–45 ft. (9–13.5 m) tall, 20 ft. (6 m) wide **Trunk(s):** 20–30 ft. (6–9 m) tall, 18 in. (45 cm) thick, covered in dark brown fibers and lighter brown leaf bases when young, mostly smooth and dark gray when older **Crownshaft:** none **Leaves:** pinnate, slightly longer than those of *Parajubaea cocoides* and more arching, with deep, glossy green 2-ft. (60-cm) long leaflets, midrib twisted so that leaflets at the outer half are vertically oriented, leaf crown normally round **Flower clusters:** sprays 3

*Parajubaea torallyi*, in Bolivia.
Martin Gibbons and Tobias Spanner

ft. (90 cm) long bearing yellow-orange unisexual flowers of both sexes **Fruit:** round, 3 in. (8 cm) wide, dark green to brown when ripe **Growth rate:** medium once past the juvenile stage **Climate:** 9b through 11 in cool but frost-free Mediterranean climes **Exposure:** sun **Soil:** any **Water needs:** low to medium **Salt tolerance:** none **Indoors:** not good **Seed germination:** slow; within two years; the very hard seed should be soaked for a few days

Because of its somewhat larger and more open crown, this species is even more attractive than *Parajubaea cocoides*.

## Pelagodoxa henryana
**Distribution:** low valley rain forest of the Marquesas Islands **Growth habit:** solitary **Height & width:** 20–30 ft. (6–9 m) tall, 12–18 ft. (4–5.4 m) wide **Trunk(s):** 15–25 ft. (4.5–7.5 m) tall, 6 in. (15 cm) thick, light brown with widely spaced rings or ridges **Crownshaft:** none **Leaves:** pinnate, 6–7 ft. (1.8–2.1 m) long, 3–4 ft. (60–90 cm) wide, undivided, deep green above, gray-

ish green beneath, on stalks 2 ft. (60 cm) long **Flower clusters:** 2-ft. (60-cm) long, sparsely branched sprays bearing yellowish unisexual flowers of both sexes **Fruit:** rounded, less than 6 in. (15 cm) wide, light brown when ripe, covered in pointed, corky conelike projections, taking several years to mature **Growth rate:** slow **Climate:** 11, marginal in 10b **Exposure:** part shade to full sun **Soil:** any but appreciates humus **Water needs:** high **Salt tolerance:** none **Indoors:** good with bright light **Seed germination:** fairly easy in a warm, moist medium; within six months

The large undivided, bicolored leaves and wonderfully round crown make this one of the world's most sought after palms. Collectors go to great lengths to cultivate this palm. Strong winds can damage the leaves.

## Phoenicophorium borsigianum
### Borsig's palm, thief's palm
**Distribution:** hills and valleys of rain forest in the Seychelles Islands **Growth habit:** solitary

*Pelagodoxa henryana*, leaf underside, in Florida.

*Pelagodoxa henryana*, fruit, in Hawaii. Chuck Hubbuch

*Phoenicophorium borsigianum*, in the Bahamas. Paul Craft

*Phoenicophorium borsigianum*, flowers, in Australia. Paul Craft

**Height & width:** 30–40 ft. (9–12 m) tall, 12–15 ft. (4–4.5 m) wide **Trunk(s):** 20–30 ft. (6–9 m) tall, 4 in. (10 cm) thick **Crownshaft:** none **Leaves:** pinnate, 6–7 ft. (1.8–2.1 m) long, but mostly undivided, usually with a V-shaped cleft at the end, heavily grooved on both surfaces, V-shaped in cross section when young but mostly flat when older, leaves and stalks of young trees covered with black spines, on yellow to orange stalks 2 ft. (60 cm) long **Flower clusters:** sprays 3 ft. (90 cm) wide bearing yellow unisexual flowers of both sexes **Fruit:** ovoid, ½ in. (12 mm) long, dull red when ripe **Growth rate:** slow to medium **Climate:** 11, marginal in warm parts of 10b **Exposure:** part shade to full sun **Soil:** any but benefits from humus **Water needs:** high **Salt tolerance:** none **Indoors:** good **Seed germination:** easy in a warm, moist medium; within a month

The gorgeous leaves are nearly incomparable in beauty, especially in young plants. The tree is one of the few solitary-trunked palms that can even look good as a single specimen, surrounded by space. Strong wind will segment the undivided leaves.

## Phoenix canariensis
### Canary Island date palm
**Distribution:** Canary Islands from sea level to 2000 ft. (600 m) elevation **Growth habit:** solitary **Height & width:** 70–90 ft. (21–27 m) tall, 25–40 ft. (7.5–12 m) wide **Trunk(s):** 50–70 ft. (15–21 m) tall, 2–3 ft. (60–90 cm) thick, brown with closely set rings of horizontally elongated diamond-shaped leaf base scars **Crownshaft:** none **Leaves:** pinnate, 10–20 ft. (3–6 m) long, with stiff, deep green leaflets, the lowest ones being long orange spines, leaf crown completely round with at least 100 leaves in it **Flower clusters:** 6-ft. (1.8-m) long sprays of yellow or orange branches bearing unisexual flowers of one sex **Fruit:** oblong, 1 in. (2.5 cm) long, light to deep orange **Growth rate:** medium to slow **Climate:** 9 through 11 in wet climes, marginal in dry parts of 8b **Exposure:** sun **Soil:** any **Water needs:** low, but grows faster and looks better

*Phoenix canariensis*, in California. Paul Craft

with regular irrigation **Salt tolerance:** fairly good **Indoors:** not good **Seed germination:** easy; within one month

Canary Island date palm has a stately elegance that no other palm can surpass. There is no finer plant for lining avenues, and a grove of this species is a wonder to behold. The tree is a beautiful and welcome sight in all but small and cramped areas. It is prone to lethal yellowing.

## Phoenix dactylifera
### Date palm, edible date palm
**Distribution:** unknown; probably the Middle East **Growth habit:** clustering **Height & width:** 70–90 ft. (21–27 m) tall, 20 ft. (6 m) wide **Trunk(s):** 40–70 ft. (12–21 m) tall, 1–2 ft. (30–60 cm) thick, brown to dark gray with closely set rings of flat "knobs" **Crownshaft:** none **Leaves:** pinnate, 10–20 ft. (3–6 m) long, slightly arching, with very stiff, rigid, grayish green to silvery green 2-ft. (60-cm) long leaflets, the lowermost leaflets as long orange spines, leaf crown hemispherical to round **Flower clusters:** 4-ft. (1.2-m) long orange sprays of whitish unisexual flowers

*Phoenix dactylifera* with ripened fruit, in Hawaii. Forest and Kim Starr, U.S. Geological Survey

*Phoenix dactylifera*, in California. Paul Craft

**Fruit:** oblong, 1–3 in. (2.5–8 cm) long, light to deep orange when ripe **Growth rate:** medium to slow **Climate:** 8b through 11 in wet climes, marginal in dry parts of 7b **Exposure:** sun **Soil:** any including alkaline media **Water needs:** low **Salt tolerance:** good **Indoors:** not good **Seed germination:** easy; within one month

Widely used for lining avenues, the date palm is often planted as a specimen tree isolated and surrounded by space. It looks better than many palms do in this situation but is even more beautiful in groups of three or more individuals of varying heights. Few other palms are better suited to being used as canopy-scapes. Date palm is slightly prone to lethal yellowing.

'Deglet Noor' is grown in Algeria, Tunisia, and the United States for its golden, semi-dry fruit that is used for baking.

'Mejhool', cultivated in Israel, Morocco, and the United States, yields a large, sweet, succulent date.

'Khadrawi' produces a soft, very dark fruit that is considered to be of the highest quality.

'Zahidi' bears medium size, cylindrical, light golden-brown semi-dry dates with a high sugar content.

## *Phoenix reclinata*
### Senegal date palm
**Distribution:** along streams and rivers in tropical Africa and Madagascar **Growth habit:** sparsely to densely clustering **Height & width:** 40–60 ft. (12–18 m) tall, 30–45 ft. (9–13.5 m) wide **Trunk(s):** 30–50 ft. (9–15 m) tall, 4–7 in. (10–18 cm) thick, always leaning to some degree, upper parts covered with dense brown fi-

*Phoenix reclinata*, in Florida.

*Phoenix reclinata*, spines (modified leaves) at leaf bases, in Florida.

*Phoenix reclinata*, a mature clump, in Florida.

bers and short leaf bases, lower parts gray with closely set rings or grooves **Crownshaft:** none **Leaves:** pinnate, 12–15 ft. (4–4.5 m) long, with stiff, glossy, deep green 1-ft. (30-cm) leaflets, the lowermost leaflets as vicious, long orange spines, leaf crown full and round **Flower clusters:** 2–3 ft. (60–90 cm) long with orange branches of unisexual flowers **Fruit:** oval, somewhat less than 1 in. (2.5 cm) long, reddish brown when ripe **Growth rate:** medium to fast **Climate:** 10 and 11, marginal in 9a **Exposure:** sun **Soil:** any but grows faster and looks better with organic matter **Water needs:** medium to high **Salt tolerance:** slight **Indoors:** good only with much space and intense light **Seed germination:** easy; within one month

The clumps are made even more graceful and dramatic if a few trunks are thinned out as the mass develops, leaving the remaining trunks of differing heights so that their individual beauty can be seen and appreciated to its fullest. If a hedge or barrier is wanted, it is best to let a few trunks of varying heights form first and then allow the many subsequent suckers to form the desired barrier at the base of the larger ones—this can be a captivating tableau. The species is slightly prone to lethal yellowing.

## Phoenix roebelinii
**Pygmy date palm, miniature date palm**
**Distribution:** along rivers in Southeast Asia **Growth habit:** solitary **Height & width:** 10–15 ft. (3–4.5 m) tall, 6–8 ft. (1.8–2.4 m) wide **Trunk(s):** 6–10 ft. (1.8–3 m) tall, 3–4 in. (8–10 cm) thick, covered in a dense mat of short brown fibers and narrow leaf bases, the oldest parts light gray with elongated "knobs" **Crownshaft:** none **Leaves:** pinnate, 3–5 ft. (90–150 cm) long, gracefully arching, with many narrow, thin, supple dark green leaflets, the lowest ones being steel-like orange spines, new growth covered in a fine white chalky bloom, leaf crown full

*Phoenix roebelinii*, in Texas. Richard Travis

*Phoenix roebelinii*, in Texas. Richard Travis

and rounded **Flower clusters:** branches 1–2 ft. (30–60 cm) long with white unisexual flowers **Fruit:** oblong, ½ in. (12 mm) long, black when ripe **Growth rate:** medium **Climate:** 9b through 11 in wet climates, marginal in dry parts of 8b **Exposure:** part shade to full sun **Soil:** appreciates organic material **Water needs:** high **Salt tolerance:** slight to none **Indoors:** good **Seed germination:** easy; within one month

Pygmy date palm is unexcelled for use as a silhouette, a small patio tree, or along a walkway where its elegance of form and detail can be appreciated up close. It is often sold in containers as a "multiple palm," meaning there are two or more individuals to a pot; this practice is encouraged as few things are lovelier than a planting of two or three of varying heights.

*Phoenix rupicola*, in California. Paul Craft

## Phoenix rupicola
### Cliff date

**Distribution:** hills and cliffs of rain forest in the Himalayan foothills of India and Bhutan **Growth habit:** solitary **Height & width:** 20–30 ft. (6–9 m) tall, 15 ft. (4.5 m) wide **Trunk(s):** 15–20 ft. (4.5–6 m) tall, 10 in. (25 cm) thick; post-juvenile stems are usually straight and gray, with closely set spirals of "knobs" **Crownshaft:** none **Leaves:** pinnate, 8–10 ft. (2.4–3 m) long, with deep green 18-in. (45-cm) long leaflets, the lowest leaflets as "soft" spines, midrib twisted so that leaflets at the outer half are vertically oriented, leaf crown full and round **Flower clusters:** 2- to 3-ft. (60- to 90-cm) long sprays of yellow unisexual flowers **Fruit:** oblong, 1 in. (2.5 cm) long, yellow-orange turning purplish brown when ripe **Growth rate:** medium **Climate:** 10 and 11 for species in wet climes, marginal in dry parts of 9b **Exposure:** part shade to full sun **Soil:** needs organic material **Water needs:** high; looks bad in dry conditions **Salt tolerance:** none **Indoors:** good with intense light and sufficient space **Seed germination:** easy; within one month

Many consider the cliff date the most beautiful date palm as it combines the grace and elegance of the miniature date palm with the nobility of the Canary Island date. A group of cliff dates with trunks of varying heights is indeed sumptuous. The tree is attractive enough to stand alone and is small enough to serve as a focal point in a large patio or courtyard, where its lushness and grace remind one of a small coconut palm. It is wonderful as a canopy-scape. Cliff date is slightly prone to lethal yellowing.

## Phoenix sylvestris
### Wild date palm, toddy palm

**Distribution:** monsoonal plains of southern Pakistan and most of India **Growth habit:** solitary **Height & width:** 50–70 ft. (15–21 m) tall, 30 ft. (9 m) wide **Trunk(s):** 40–50 ft. (12–15 m) tall, 18 in. (45 cm) thick, often covered in broadly triangular leaf bases when younger, light to dark gray or brown with closely set spirals of "knobs" when older or weathered **Crownshaft:** none

**Leaves:** pinnate, slightly plumose, 8–10 ft. (2.4–3 cm) long, with stiff, grayish to bluish green 18-in. (45-cm) long leaflets, leaf crown round and packed with as many as 100 leaves **Flower clusters:** 3-ft. long sprays of yellow branches bearing unisexual flowers **Fruit:** oblong, 1 in. (2.5 cm) long, purplish red when ripe **Growth rate:** medium to fast **Climate:** 9 through 11 **Exposure:** sun **Soil:** any **Water needs:** low, but grows faster and looks better with regular irrigation **Salt tolerance:** medium **Indoors:** not good **Seed germination:** easy; within one month

This species is similar to *Phoenix canariensis* but is smaller with a more compact crown and usually grows significantly faster. It can be planted to line avenues or in groves. Wild date palm is slightly prone to lethal yellowing.

## Phoenix theophrasti
### Cretan date palm

**Distribution:** at springs and seepages in coastal Crete, southeastern Greece, and southwestern Turkey **Growth habit:** freely clustering **Height & width:** 40–60 ft. (12–18 m) tall, 20–30 ft. (6–9 m) wide **Trunk(s):** 20–30 ft. (6–9 m) tall, 1½–2 ft. (45–60 cm) thick, usually covered in light gray, widely triangular leaf bases **Crownshaft:** none **Leaves:** pinnate, 10–15 ft. (3–4.5 m) long, slightly arching, with very stiff, rigid, silvery gray to almost completely blue 2-ft. (60-cm) long leaflets, the lowermost leaflets as long orange spines, leaf crown hemispherical to round with only 20–40 leaves **Flower clusters:** 3-ft. (90-cm) long sprays of yellow branches bearing unisexual flowers **Fruit:** similar to those of *Phoenix dactylifera*

*Phoenix sylvestris*, in California. Paul Craft

*Phoenix theophrasti*, in Florida. Richard Travis

*Pinanga caesia*, new leaf color, in Florida.

*Pinanga caesia*, flowers, in Costa Rica. Paul Craft

but smaller and not as brightly colored **Growth rate:** slow **Climate:** 9 through 11 in wet climes, 8 through 11 in dry climes **Exposure:** sun **Soil:** any including alkaline media **Water needs:** low **Salt tolerance:** high **Indoors:** not good **Seed germination:** easy; within one month

This palm may be a shorter, more clustering form of the edible date palm, with shorter, more bristly leaves. It can be used for the same landscape purposes: lining avenues, as an isolated specimen or in groups of three or more, or as a canopy-scape. It is slightly prone to lethal yellowing.

## Pinanga caesia

**Distribution:** low mountainous rain forest of Sulawesi **Growth habit:** solitary **Height & width:** 12–18 ft. (4–5.4 m) tall, 6–8 ft. (1.8–2.4 m) wide **Trunk(s):** 8–12 ft. (2.4–4 m) tall, 3 in. (8 cm) thick, dark green with wavy light brown rings **Crownshaft:** 18 in. (45 cm) tall, brownish orange, smooth, bulging at the base **Leaves:** pinnate, 5–6 ft. (1.5–1.8 m) long, slightly arching, with widely spaced, deep green, linear limp leaflets, the apical pair wider, new growth golden to brownish pink **Flower clusters:** sprays of 1- to 1½-ft. (30- to 45-cm) long pendent coral branches turning red and bearing unisexual flowers of both sexes **Fruit:** round, ½ in. (12 mm) wide, deep red when ripe **Growth rate:** medium **Climate:** 10b and 11 **Exposure:** part shade **Soil:** needs organic material **Water needs:** high **Salt tolerance:** none **Indoors:** good **Seed germination:** easy in a warm, moist medium; within one month

Amazingly attractive, *Pinanga caesia* is among the most colorful palms.

## Pinanga coronata
### Ivory cane palm

**Synonym:** *Pinanga kuhlii* **Distribution:** low mountainous rain forest of Indonesia **Growth habit:** clustering **Height & width:** 10–25 ft. (3–7.5 m) tall, 15 ft. (4.5 m) wide **Trunk(s):** 6–20 ft. (1.8–6 m) tall, 2 in. (5 cm) thick, dark green with dark brown rings **Crownshaft:** 1 ft. (30 cm) tall, slightly thicker than the trunk, yellow to light green, cylindrical **Leaves:** pinnate, 4–5 ft. (1.2–

*Pinanga coronata*, fruit, in Cuba. Paul Craft

1.5 m) long, on 1-ft. (30-cm) long stalks, with light to deep green leaflets varying from narrow and pointed to wide with squared and jagged ends, new growth often suffused with pink or red, leaf crown with four to six leaves **Flower clusters:** sprays of 1-ft. (30-cm) long pink branches turning red and bearing white unisexual flowers of both sexes **Fruit:** ovoid, ½ in. (12 mm) long, glossy black when ripe **Growth rate:** medium **Climate:** 10b and 11, marginal in 10a **Exposure:** part shade, especially in hot climates **Soil:** needs organic material **Water needs:** high **Salt tolerance:** none **Indoors:** very good **Seed germination:** easy in a warm, moist medium; within one month

Ivory cane palm makes a beautiful small hedge or wall in semishady sites. It is a near perfect accent in borders and is unsurpassed in intimate patios and courtyard plantings.

## Pinanga dicksonii
**Distribution:** wet forest of Ghat Mountains in India at 1000 ft. (300 m) elevation **Growth habit:** clustering **Height & width:** 15–30 ft. (4.5–9 m) tall and wide **Trunk(s):** 10–25 ft. (3–7.5 m) tall,

*Pinanga coronata*, in Florida.

2 in. (5 cm) thick, deep green with widely spaced deep gray rings **Crownshaft:** 2 ft. (60 cm) tall, as thick as the trunk, golden, cylindrical, smooth **Leaves:** pinnate, 4–6 ft. (1.2–1.8 m) long, on very short stalks, spreading but hardly arching, with linear, pointed, grassy to emerald green 2-ft. (60-cm) long pendent leaflets **Flower clusters:** sprays of 1-ft. (30-cm) long gold branches turning coral and bearing pink unisexual flowers of both sexes **Fruit:** round, ½ in. (12 mm) wide, deep red when ripe **Growth rate:** medium to fast **Climate:** 10 and 11 **Exposure:** part shade **Soil:** needs organic material **Water needs:** high **Salt tolerance:** none **Indoors:** very good with enough space **Seed germination:** easy in a warm, moist medium; within one month

*Pinanga maculata*, crownshaft, in Australia. Paul Craft

*Pinanga dicksonii*, in Florida.

Resembling a giant *Chamaedorea* species, *Pinanga dicksonii* has unsurpassed gracefulness and color.

## Pinanga maculata

**Distribution:** low mountainous rain forest of the Philippine Islands **Growth habit:** solitary **Height & width:** 18–30 ft. (5.4–9 m) tall, 6 ft. (1.8 m) wide **Trunk(s):** 10–20 ft. (3–6 m) tall, 4–6 in. (10–15 cm) thick **Crownshaft:** 18 in. (45 cm) tall, slightly thicker than the trunk, reddish brown to purplish brown, slightly bulging **Leaves:** pinnate, 4 ft. (1.2 m) long, with thick, heavily veined leaflets that have jagged ends and are dark green above and silvery beneath **Flower clusters:** sprays of 1- to 2-ft. (30- to 60-cm) long yellowish branches bearing unisexual flowers of both sexes **Fruit:** oval with a

*Pinanga maculata*, leaf, in Australia. Paul Craft

*Pinanga maculata*, in Australia. Paul Craft

beak, 1 in. (2.5 cm) long, purple to black when ripe **Growth rate:** medium **Climate:** 10 and 11 **Exposure:** part shade **Soil:** humus laden and moist **Water needs:** high **Salt tolerance:** none **Indoors:** perfect with high humidity **Seed germination:** easy in a warm, moist medium; within one month

This is one of the world's most beautiful small palms; each individual is a little symphony of color and form and needs to be placed where its intimate beauty can be appreciated up close.

## Pinanga patula

**Distribution:** low mountainous rain forest of peninsular Sumatra, peninsular Malaysia, and Indonesian Borneo **Growth habit:** solitary, occasionally clustering **Height & width:** usually 19 ft. (5.7 m) tall but sometimes only 15 ft. (4.5 m), 6–9 ft. (1.8–3 m) **Trunk(s):** 10–12 ft. (3–4 m) tall, slightly more than 1 in. (2.5 cm) thick, dark green with light green rings **Crownshaft:** 2 ft.

(60 cm) tall, as thick as the trunk, yellow-orange to almost white **Leaves:** pinnate, 3 ft. (90 cm) long, with closely set, strongly ribbed, light to dark green leaflets, the outer ones squared off and with jagged ends **Flower clusters:** small, wiry, sparsely branched, yellow, bearing unisexual flowers of both sexes **Fruit:** oval with a point, 1 in. (2.5 cm) long, red, brown, or black **Growth rate:** medium to slow **Climate:** 10b and 11 **Exposure:** part shade **Soil:** humus laden and moist **Water needs:** high **Salt tolerance:** none **Indoors:** very good with high humidity **Seed germination:** easy in a warm, moist medium; within one month

This species is especially choice because of its large, impressive, rounded, and heavy leaf crown.

## Pritchardia hillebrandii

**Distribution:** Molokai, Hawaii **Growth habit:** solitary **Height & width:** 18–30 ft. (5.4–9 m) tall, 10–15 ft. (3–4.5 m) wide **Trunk(s):** 12–20 ft. (4–6 m) tall, 10–12 in. (25–30 cm) thick **Crownshaft:** none **Leaves:** palmate, wedge- to

*Pinanga patula*, in Venezuela. Paul Craft

*Pritchardia hillebrandii*, leaf, in Florida.

*Pritchardia hillebrandii*, in Hawaii. Chuck Hubbuch

diamond-shaped, 4 ft. (1.2 m) long, with deeply pleated, dark green to bluish green to nearly blue leaflets and slightly wavy margins, on thick 3-ft. (90-cm) long, chalk-covered, whitish stalks **Flower clusters:** short yellow branches at the ends of the stems that are slightly longer than the radius of the leaf crown bearing bisexual flowers **Fruit:** round, 1–2 in. (2.5–5 cm) wide, dark brown to black when ripe **Growth rate:** slow **Climate:** 10 and 11, marginal in warmest parts of 9b **Exposure:** part shade to full sun **Soil:** any but faster growing and better looking with organic material **Water needs:** medium **Salt tolerance:** none **Indoors:** only with bright light and very good air circulation **Seed germination:** easy and quick if fresh; within a month

All *Pritchardia* species are susceptible to lethal yellowing and should be planted in disease-free areas only.

## Pritchardia pacifica
### Fiji fan palm, Pacific fan palm
**Distribution:** coastal areas of the Tonga Islands **Growth habit:** solitary **Height & width:** 30–40 ft. (9–12 m) tall, 12 ft. (4 m) wide **Trunk(s):**

20–30 ft. (6–9 m) tall, 1 ft. (30 cm) thick, light gray to pure white, smooth for the most part **Crownshaft:** none **Leaves:** palmate, wedge- to diamond-shaped, 3–6 ft. (90–180 cm) wide, with stiff, rigid, very dark green, deeply pleated leaflets, on thick white stalks 5–7 ft. (1.5–2.1 m) long **Flower clusters:** short yellow branches at the ends of 3- to 5-ft. (90- to 150-cm) long stalks bearing bisexual flowers **Fruit:** round, ½–1 in. (6–12 mm) wide, a deep, glossy black when ripe **Growth rate:** medium **Climate:** 10b and 11, marginal in warmest parts of 10a **Exposure:** full sun to part shade **Soil:** any, including alkaline media **Water needs:** medium, but drought tolerant when established **Salt tolerance:** medium **Indoors:** only with bright light and very good air circulation **Seed germination:** easy and quick if fresh; within a month

This species is among the world's most beautiful and tropical-looking fan palms.

## Pritchardia thurstonii
### Thurston palm, Thurston fan palm
**Distribution:** coastal regions of the Fiji Islands **Growth habit:** solitary **Height & width:** 25–45

*Pritchardia pacifica*, in New Caledonia. Paul Craft

ft. (7.5–13.5 m) tall, 10–15 ft. (3–4.5 m) wide **Trunk(s):** 20–40 ft. (6–9 m) tall, 8–12 in. (20–30 cm) thick **Crownshaft:** none **Leaves:** palmate, semicircular to diamond-shaped, 4–6 ft. (1.2–1.8 m) wide, with medium to deep green pleated leaflets on stems 3 ft. (90 cm) long **Flower clusters:** 10-ft. (3-m) long stems at the ends of which are short yellow branches projecting out and down from the leaf crown bearing bisexual flowers **Fruit:** round, ½–1 in. (6–12 mm) wide, deep red to black when ripe **Growth rate:** slow to medium **Climate:** 10 and 11 **Exposure:** full sun **Soil:** any but relishes alkaline media **Water needs:** medium to low **Salt tolerance:** good **Indoors:** only with much light and good air circulation **Seed germination:** easy and quick if fresh; within a month

Like the Fiji fan palm, this palm has a beautiful silhouette and is even more tolerant of seaside conditions.

## Pseudophoenix lediniana

**Distribution:** southwestern Haiti **Growth habit:** solitary **Height & width:** 30–50 ft. (9–15 m) tall, 15–20 ft. (4.5–6 m) wide **Trunk(s):** 30–50 ft. (9–15 m) tall, 1 ft. (30 cm) thick, light greenish gray to almost white with widely spaced deep green rings **Crownshaft:** 2–3 ft. (90 cm) tall, bluish to grayish green, smooth, waxy, tapering **Leaves:** pinnate, 12 ft. (4 m) long, with many somewhat limp dark green leaflets growing in a flat plane, on short, thick stalks **Flower clusters:** 4 ft. (1.2 m) long and much branched, bearing yellowish white bisexual flowers **Fruit:** round, 1 in. (2.5 cm) wide, deep red when ripe **Growth rate:** medium **Climate:** 10 and 11 **Exposure:** sun **Soil:** any but relishes alkaline media **Water needs:** medium **Salt tolerance:** small **Indoors:** only with intense light and good air circulation **Seed germination:** difficult; from 2 to 12 months; seed should be left to dry out for two to four weeks, the shell cracked, after which the seed should be soaked in water for two days and then planted in perlite, with bottom heat

This species has one of the palm world's most beautiful trunks and crownshafts, reminiscent of a more colorful royal palm.

*Pritchardia thurstonii*, in Florida. Paul Craft

*Pseudophoenix lediniana*, in Florida.

## *Pseudophoenix sargentii*
### Buccaneer palm, cherry palm

**Distribution:** Florida Keys, northern Caribbean islands and coasts **Growth habit:** solitary **Height & width:** 20–40 ft. (6–12 m) tall, 12 ft. (4 m) wide **Trunk(s):** 15–25 ft. (4.5–7.5 m) tall, 1 ft. (30 cm) thick, with a bulge at midpoint or above, gray green to light gray with dark green to brown rings in the upper part, light to dark gray with indistinct rings in the lower part **Crownshaft:** usually loose and indistinct in younger palms, 12–24 in. (30–60 cm) tall, light gray green to almost white, smooth, waxy, slightly bulging and tapering on older trees **Leaves:** pinnate, 8 ft. (2.4 m) long, shallowly V-shaped in cross section, with dark to bluish green leaflets, on stout 2-ft. (60-cm) long stalks **Flower clusters:** 3–4 ft. (90–120 cm) long with many short branches bearing small yellow bisexual and unisexual flowers **Fruit:** round, ½ in. (12 mm) wide, deep red when ripe **Growth

*Pseudophoenix sargentii*, an old tree, in Florida.

*Pseudophoenix sargentii*, flowers. Paul Craft

rate: slow **Climate:** 9b through 11, marginal in warmest parts of 9a **Exposure:** sun **Soil:** any but relishes alkaline media **Water needs:** medium to low **Salt tolerance:** high **Indoors:** only with bright light and good air circulation **Seed germination:** difficult; from 2 to 12 months; seed should be left to dry out for two to four weeks, the shell cracked, after which the seed should be soaked in water for two days and then planted in perlite, with bottom heat

Buccaneer palm is an excellent choice for seashores as well as intimate sites like patios and courtyards.

## Ptychosperma caryotoides

**Distribution:** low mountainous rain forest of eastern Papua New Guinea **Growth habit:** solitary **Height & width:** 20–35 ft. (6–10.5 m) tall, 6–9 ft. (1.8–2.7 m) wide **Trunk(s):** 20–30 ft. (6–9 m) tall, 1–3 in. (2.5–8 cm) thick, light gray with indistinct rings **Crownshaft:** 1 ft. (30 cm) tall,

nearly white, slightly bulging at the top **Leaves:** pinnate, 2–5 ft. (60–150 cm) long, with widely spaced dark green wedge-shaped leaflets that have jagged ends **Flower clusters:** 1–2 ft. (30–60 cm) long, sparsely branched, bearing unisexual flowers of both sexes **Fruit:** round, small, bright red when ripe **Growth rate:** medium to slow **Climate:** 10b and 11, marginal in warmest parts of 10a **Exposure:** part shade **Soil:** humus laden and moist **Water needs:** medium to high **Salt tolerance:** none **Indoors:** good **Seed germination:** easy and quick in a warm, moist medium

Despite its name, this palm only superficially resembles fishtail palms in the genus *Caryota*.

## Ptychosperma elegans
### Solitaire palm

**Distribution:** rain forests of eastern Queensland, Australia **Growth habit:** solitary **Height & width:** 25–40 ft. (7.5–12 m) tall, 8–12 ft. (2.4–4 m) wide **Trunk(s):** 20–35 ft. (6–10.5 m) tall, 4

*Ptychosperma caryotoides*, in Florida.

*Ptychosperma elegans*, in Florida.

*Ptychosperma elegans*, crownshaft, stem, and fruit.

in. (10 cm) thick, light gray to white with distinct, widely spaced dark green or brown rings **Crownshaft:** 2 ft. (60 cm) tall, silvery gray to silver-green, slightly bulging at the base **Leaves:** pinnate, 6–8 ft. (1.8–2.4 m) long, shallowly V-shaped in cross section, with many 2-ft. (60-cm) long leaflets with jagged ends, dark green above and pale green beneath **Flower clusters:** 2–3 ft. (60–90 cm) long with greenish yellow branches bearing white unisexual flowers of both sexes **Fruit:** ovoid, 1 in. (2.5 cm) long, bright red when ripe **Growth rate:** medium to fast **Climate:** 10b and 11, marginal in warmest parts of 10a **Exposure:** part shade to full sun **Soil:** any but faster growing and better looking with moist, humus-laden media; tolerates alkaline media **Water needs:** medium to high **Salt tolerance:** slight **Indoors:** good with bright light and high humidity **Seed germination:** easy and quick in a warm, moist medium

The tree is of unsurpassed grace, symmetry, and beauty of form and is even more exquisite when planted in groups of three individuals of varying heights. Its silhouette is lovely and notable enough that it should be called the silhouette

palm. All *Ptychosperma* species have fruits with highly irritating juice.

## *Ptychosperma macarthurii*
### Macarthur palm

**Distribution:** rain forests and swamps of southern Papua New Guinea and adjacent northeastern Queensland, Australia **Growth habit:** clustering, with few to many stems in a clump **Height & width:** 30–40 ft. (9–12 m) tall, 15–25 ft. (4.5–7.5 m) wide **Trunk(s):** 15–25 ft. (4.5–7.5 m) tall, 2 in. (5 cm) thick, light tan to light gray **Crownshaft:** 1–2 ft. (30–60 cm) tall, light green, slightly bulging at the base **Leaves:** pinnate, 3–6 ft. (90–180 cm) long, with 2-ft. (60-cm) long, narrow, dark green leaflets with jagged ends, on short stalks **Flower clusters:** 2 ft. (60 cm) long, with many yellowish green branches bearing yellowish white unisexual flowers of both sexes **Fruit:** ovoid, ½ in. (12 mm) long, light to deep red when ripe **Growth rate:** medium to rather fast **Climate:** 10b and 11, marginal in warmest parts of 10a **Exposure:** part shade to full sun **Soil:** humus laden and fairly moist; tolerates calcareous media **Water needs:** high

*Ptychosperma macarthurii*, in the Dominican Republic. Paul Craft

*Ptychosperma macarthurii*, fruit, in Belize. Paul Craft

Salt tolerance: little **Indoors:** good with intense light and high humidity **Seed germination:** easy and quick in a warm, moist medium

The Macarthur palm can be used with or without its suckers. When grown without the suckers and underplanted with smaller vegetation, such as *Chamaedorea* palms, the beautifully ringed trunks are visible. When grown with the suckers, however, a sumptuous wall of tiered leaves is created. Either method creates a wonderful tableau of tropical luxuriance.

## Raphia australis

**Distribution:** swampy areas of southeastern Mozambique and northeastern South Africa **Growth habit:** solitary **Height & width:** 50–80 ft. (15–24 m) tall, 30–40 ft. (9–12 m) wide **Trunk(s):** 20–40 ft. (6–12 m) tall, 18 in. (45 cm) thick **Crownshaft:** none **Leaves:** pinnate, 30–60 ft. (9–18 m) long, erect, ascending, and only slightly arching, with

*Raphia australis*, in Australia. Paul Craft

stiff, 2- to 3-ft. (60- to 90-ft.) long, pointed deep green to deep bluish green leaflets growing at different angles from the massive orange midrib to create a nearly plumose effect, on massively thick, 3-ft. (90-cm) long orange stalks **Flower clusters:** 10–12 ft. (3–4 m) long, shortly branched and congested, bearing unisexual flowers of both sexes, arising from the growing point atop the tree, which slowly dies after the fruits are mature **Fruit:** round, 3–4 in. (8–10 cm) wide, gray to light brown, with overlapping scales **Growth rate:** fast once past the seedling stage **Climate:** 10b and 11, marginal in warmest parts of 10a **Exposure:** part shade to full sun **Soil:** any but tolerates calcareous media **Water needs:** high **Salt tolerance:** slight **Indoors:** good with much space, light, and moisture **Seed germination:** easy; within one to two months in a warm, moist medium

Trees live an average of 40 years.

## Raphia farinifera

**Distribution:** rain forests and swamps of Uganda, Kenya, and Tanzania **Growth habit:** usually solitary, occasionally clustering **Height & width:** 50–80 ft. (15–24 m) tall and wide **Trunk(s):** 6–30 ft. (1.8–9 m) tall, 2 ft. (60 cm) thick **Crownshaft:** none **Leaves:** pinnate, plumose, 40–70 ft. (12–21 m) long, with numerous 6- to 8-ft. (1.8- to 2.4-m) long narrow leaflets that are deep green above and waxy bluish beneath, growing from the massive orange midrib at different angles, on massive orange stalks 6–20 ft. (1.8–6 m) long **Flower clusters:** 10 ft. (3 m) long, ropelike, growing from the top of the tree, narrow with large, yellow overlapping bracts covering yellowish white to orange unisexual flowers of both sexes **Fruit:** top-shaped, 3–4 in. (8–10 cm) long, shiny mahogany colored overlapping scales **Growth rate:** fast once past the seedling stage **Climate:** 10b and 11 **Exposure:** sun **Soil:** any moist media; tolerates calcareous media **Water needs:** high **Salt tolerance:** little **Indoors:** only with an extraordinarily large space and much light and moisture **Seed germination:** easy; within one to two months in a warm, moist medium

*Raphia farinifera*, fruit, in Florida.

The gargantuan trunk dies slowly after fruits mature, but individual stems usually live for 40 to 60 years.

## Ravenea glauca

**Distribution:** low mountainous dry evergreen forests of central Madagascar **Growth habit:** solitary **Height & width:** 15–25 ft. (4.5–7.5 m) tall, 8 ft. (2.4 m) wide **Trunk(s):** 10–20 ft. (3–6 m) tall, 3–4 in. (8–10 cm) thick **Crownshaft:** none **Leaves:** pinnate, 4–6 ft. (1.2–1.8 m) long, with many very narrow, pointed, regularly spaced dark green leaflets that are mostly erect and stiff when young but softer and more pendent when older **Flower clusters:** 1 ft. (30 cm) long, sparsely branched, bearing yellow-green unisexual flowers **Fruit:** round, ½ in. (12 mm) wide, deep yellow when ripe **Growth rate:** medium to slow **Climate:** 10 and 11, survives in warm and dry parts of 9b, best in Mediterranean climes **Exposure:** part shade to sun **Soil:** any **Water needs:** low **Salt tolerance:** slight **Indoors:** good with enough light **Seed germination:** easy and fairly quick if fresh

*Ravenea glauca.* Rolf Kyburz

*Ravenea rivularis*, in Florida.

This species resembles a miniature majesty palm. New growth is glaucous, hence the species name.

## *Ravenea rivularis*
### Majesty palm, majestic palm

**Distribution:** along rivers and in swamps of central and southern Madagascar **Growth habit:** solitary **Height & width:** 30–50 ft. (9–15 m) tall, 12–15 ft. (4–4.5 m) wide **Trunk(s):** 15–40 ft. (4.5–12 m) tall, 12–15 in. (4–4.5 m) thick, swollen at the base, gray to nearly white **Crownshaft:** none **Leaves:** pinnate, 6–8 ft. (1.8–2.4 m) long, on thick, short stems, with many narrow, dark green leaflets, the midrib twists at the midpoint so that leaflets at the outer half are oriented vertically **Flower clusters:** 2–3 ft. (60–90 cm) long, with many yellow-green branches bearing whitish unisexual flowers **Fruit:** round, ½ in. (12 mm) wide, bright red when ripe **Growth rate:** fast in optimum growing conditions **Climate:** 10 and 11 **Exposure:** part shade to full sun **Soil:** rich, humus laden and moist **Water needs:** high **Salt tolerance:** none **Indoors:** good with high humidity year-round and bright light **Seed germination:** easy and fairly quick if fresh

It is difficult if not impossible to give this palm too much water. It is attractive enough to be used as a specimen tree, but looks better in groups of three or more trees of varying heights. Majestic palm is often grown in containers.

## *Reinhardtia gracilis*
### Window palm, windowpane palm

**Distribution:** understory of rain forests in Central America **Growth habit:** mostly clustering,

*Reinhardtia gracilis*, in California. Barry Osborne

occasionally solitary **Height & width:** 5–12 ft. (1.5–4 m) tall, 4–6 ft. (1.2–1.8 m) wide **Trunk(s):** 6–10 ft. (1.8–3 m) tall, 1 in. (2.5 cm) thick, upper parts covered with brownish parchment-like wrapping of old leaf bases, lower parts dark green with lighter colored rings **Crownshaft:** none **Leaves:** pinnate, 8–12 in. (20–30 cm) long, on stalks 3–24 in. (8–60 cm) long, with four to eight paired leaflets along the wiry midrib, the outermost pair larger than the others, each wedge-shaped leaflet with strong ribs and four to six elliptical "windows" at the base **Flower clusters:** thin, tail-like pendent spikes of whitish unisexual flowers of both sexes **Fruit:** round, ¼ in. (6 mm) wide, black when ripe **Growth rate:** slow **Climate:** 10b and 11, marginal in warmest parts of 10a **Exposure:** bright shade to part shade **Soil:** humus laden and moist **Water needs:** medium **Salt tolerance:** none **Indoors:** perfect with high humidity **Seed germination:** easy; within 45 days with moisture and warmth

Because of its small size, this palm is suitable only for an intimate site in which it can be seen up close. It is perfect for containers on a shaded patio or courtyard.

## *Reinhardtia latisecta*
### Giant windowpane palm
**Distribution:** understory of rain forests in Central America **Growth habit:** clustering **Height & width:** 15 ft. (5 m) tall and wide, sometimes up to 25 ft. (7.5 m) tall **Trunk(s):** 10–20 ft. (3–6 m) tall, 2 in. (5 cm) thick, upper parts dark green with darker rings **Crownshaft:** none **Leaves:** pinnate, 3–5 ft. (90–150 cm) long, with four to six pairs of unequally sized deep green, ribbed leaflets, the outermost pair wider than the others, and with four to six narrow slits or "windows" at the base of each leaflet **Flower clusters:** pale, thin branches 8 in. (20 cm) long radiating from the ends of stems 3 ft. (90 cm) long, turning reddish, and bearing small unisexual flowers of both

*Reinhardtia latisecta*. Rolf Kyburz

*Reinhardtia latisecta*, leaf showing "windows."
Rolf Kyburz

sexes **Fruit:** round, ½ in. (12 mm) wide, black when ripe **Growth rate:** slow to medium **Climate:** 10b and 11 **Exposure:** part shade **Soil:** humus laden and moist **Water needs:** high **Salt tolerance:** none **Indoors:** good with bright light and constantly high humidity **Seed germination:** easy; within 45 days if given moisture and warmth

This is the most beautiful species in the genus. Its size assures that it will not be lost among other vegetation and its large, matte green, shapely leaves are a delight up close and from afar. Its only fault is its intolerance of cold.

## *Rhapidophyllum hystrix*
### Needle palm, vegetable porcupine

**Distribution:** as an undergrowth plant in southern Mississippi, southern Alabama, northwestern and northern peninsular Florida, and southern coastal South Carolina **Growth habit:** clustering **Height & width:** 5–12 ft. tall (1.5–4 m) tall, 6–8 ft. (1.8–2.4 m) wide **Trunk(s):** 3–6 ft. (90–180 cm) tall, 4 in. (10 cm) thick, but appearing much thicker because of the adherent mass of fibers and leaf bases, the growing point surrounded by a dense mass of 8- to 16-in. (20- to 40-cm) long needlelike fibers **Crownshaft:** none **Leaves:** palmate, semicircular to circular, 4 ft. (1.2 m) wide, with deep green, pointed segments extending almost to the stalk, which is 3–5 ft. (90–150 cm) long **Flower clusters:** short, stubby, and sparsely branched, bearing yellowish white to pale lavender usually bisexual flowers but sometimes all male or all female **Fruit:** round, ½ in. (12 mm) wide, brown to reddish purple, covered in very short white hairs **Growth rate:** slow **Climate:** 6b through 11, probably the world's hardiest palm species **Exposure:** part shade to full sun, producing longer leaf stalks, wider leaves, and a more open and elegant appearance with less dense clustering in shade **Soil:** humus laden and moist **Water needs:** medium to high **Salt tolerance:** none **Indoors:** unknown **Seed germination:** slow and sporadic; needs a container at least 6 in. (15 cm) deep

This palm looks its best if grown in shade with most of its suckers removed, which procedure

*Rhapidophyllum hystrix*, in habitat at Torreya State Park in northwestern Florida.

allows one to see the beautiful form of the leaf crown. It makes an excellent specimen in small gardens, and its infamous needles are usually no problem as they are almost hidden in the center of the leaf crown. Needle palm can also be used to form an impenetrable low hedge.

## *Rhapis excelsa*
### Lady palm, tall lady palm

**Distribution:** never found in the wild but presumably from limestone hills and cliffs of southern China and Taiwan **Growth habit:** clustering **Height & width:** 8–12 ft. (2.4–4 m) tall, 6–12 ft. (1.8–4 m) wide **Trunk(s):** 6–10 ft. (1.8–3 m) tall, 1 in. (2.5 cm) thick, covered in a tight wrap of wovenlike black fibers **Crownshaft:** none **Leaves:** palmate, circular, with narrow, ribbed dark green segments extending to the wiry, 18-in. (45-cm) long stalks **Flower clusters:** short, brushlike, with yellowish white branches bearing unisexual flowers **Fruit:** round, small, white when ripe **Growth rate:** slow **Climate:** 9 through 11, marginal in warmest parts of 8b **Exposure:** part shade, especially in hot climates **Soil:** any with excellent drainage; tolerates calcareous media **Water needs:** medium **Salt tolerance:** none **Indoors:** excellent **Seed germination:** easy; within four months; needs a container at least 6 in. (15 cm) deep

That the leaves grow from the trunks for most of the trunk length and that the new canes or trunks grow mostly from the perimeter of a clump make this little palm species near perfection for informal tall hedge material in partially

*Rhapis excelsa* and a variegated-leaved form of *Dracaena fragrans* at Moody Gardens in Galveston, Texas.

shaded sites. It is also almost unexcelled as a close-up specimen where its grace can be fully appreciated; like many other clumping palm species, it is more graceful and artistic if some of the crowded trunks are removed to better show off its wonderful silhouette. Few plants are as beautiful near water as is the lady palm.

## Rhapis humilis
### Slender lady palm

**Distribution:** unknown in the wild but presumably from limestone hills and cliffs of southern China and Taiwan **Growth habit:** clustering **Height & width:** 15–25 ft. (4.5–7.5 m) tall, 8 ft. (2.4 m) wide **Trunk(s):** 12–20 ft. (4–6 m) tall, 1 in. (2.5 cm) thick, upper part wrapped in woven-like black fibers, most of length dark green with lighter colored rings **Crownshaft:** none **Leaves:** palmate, nearly circular, 24–30 in. (60–75 cm) wide, with many narrow, deep green, pointed segments extending to the 2-ft. (60-cm) long, wiry stalks **Flower clusters:** short, brushlike, with yellowish white branches bearing unisexual flowers similar to those of *Rhapis excelsa* **Fruit:** round, small, white when ripe **Growth rate:** slow **Climate:** 8b through 11, marginal in 8a, better in Mediterranean climes than in hot and humid ones **Exposure:** part shade to full sun **Soil:** any with excellent drainage; tolerates calcareous media **Water needs:** moderate **Salt tolerance:** none **Indoors:** excellent with enough light and good air circulation **Seed germination:** easy; within four months; needs a container at least 6 in. (15 cm) deep

This species is, if possible, more beautiful than the large lady palm: it is taller and more elegant

*Rhapis humilis*, in California.

looking, and its softer, larger leaves are even more appealing. As a giant hedge or barrier, slender lady palm is unexcelled, and its silhouette is as lovely as that of any palm species. The only landscape situation it is not perfectly suited to is that of a specimen planting surrounded by space, and even there it is good if its silhouette is against a wall or contrasting vegetation.

## Rhapis multifida

**Distribution:** monsoonal evergreen forests of southern China on limestone soils **Growth habit:** sparsely clustering **Height & width:** 6 ft. (1.8 m) tall and wide, sometimes up to 10 ft. (3 m) tall **Trunk(s):** 4–8 ft. (1.2–2.4 m) tall, less than 1 in. (2.5 cm) thick **Crownshaft:** none **Leaves:** palmate, semicircular, 2 ft. (60 cm) wide, with 12 to 24 quite narrow medium green segments that extend almost to the 18-in. (45-cm) long wiry stalks **Flower clusters:** 18-in. (45-cm) long, erect, broomlike yellowish felt-covered branches bearing unisexual flowers **Fruit:** round, about ¼ in. (6 mm) wide, black when ripe **Growth rate:** slow **Climate:** 9b through 11 **Exposure:** part shade **Soil:** any but loves calcareous media **Water needs:** moderate **Salt tolerance:** none **Indoors:** good in bright light **Seed germination:** easy; within four months; needs a container at least 6 in. (15 cm) deep

This very graceful, fine-leaved species is greatly underused and deserves much greater appreciation and availability. Its small delicate silhouette is thrilling.

## Rhopalostylis baueri
### Norfolk Island palm, Norfolk Island shaving brush palm

**Distribution:** low mountainous subtropical rain forest of Norfolk Island in the South Pacific **Growth habit:** solitary **Height & width:** 30–50 ft. (9–15 m) tall, 10–15 ft. (3–4.5 m) wide **Trunk(s):** 25–50 ft. (7.5–15 m) tall, 8 in. (20 cm) thick, light to dark green in all but oldest parts, with very closely set tan to gray rings **Crownshaft:** 3 ft. (90 cm) tall, light yellow-green, cylindrical, bulging at the base **Leaves:** pinnate, 12 ft. (4 m) long, erect and ascending, V-shaped in cross section, the stout midrib nearly white, with many light to dark green pointed, 2- to 3-ft. (60- to 90-cm) long leaflets **Flower clusters:** 3 ft. (90 cm) long, with numerous tan to brown branches growing from beneath the crownshaft and bearing small unisexual flowers of both sexes **Fruit:** ovoid, ½ in. (12 mm) long, reddish when ripe **Growth rate:** slow as a juvenile, medium thereafter **Climate:** 9b through 11 in cool but frostless Mediterranean climes **Exposure:** part shade to full sun in cooler Mediterranean climes **Soil:** humus laden and moist **Water needs:** medium to high **Salt tolerance:** little **Indoors:** good with very bright light, adequate air circulation, and humidity **Seed germination:** easy; within two months if fresh

*Rhapis multifida*, in Florida.

*Rhopalostylis baueri,* in California. Barry Osborne

*Rhopalostylis sapida*, in California. Barry Osborne

This tall palm has a distinctly smooth, ringed trunk and a narrow, erect crown shaped like a shaving brush. It is intolerant of cold and impossible to grow in hot, tropical climates.

## Rhopalostylis sapida
### Nikau palm, shaving brush palm, feather duster palm

**Distribution:** low mountainous temperate rain forests of New Zealand and the Chatham Islands **Growth habit:** solitary **Height & width:** 25–40 ft. (7.5–12 m) tall, 15–25 ft. (4.5–7.5 m) wide **Trunk(s):** 20–30 ft. (6–9 m) tall, 8–10 in. (20–25 cm) thick **Crownshaft:** 2–3 ft. (60–90 cm) tall, yellowish green, tapering, very plump and bulbous, much swollen **Leaves:** pinnate, 16 ft. (4.8 m) long, erect and ascending, shallowly V-shaped in cross section, the stout midrib almost white, with 2- to 3-ft. (60- to 90-cm) long, stiff dark green pointed leaflets **Flower clusters:** 2- to 3-ft. (60- to 90-cm) long sprays of yellowish brown branches bearing light purple unisexual flowers of both sexes **Fruit:** round, ½ in. (12 mm) wide, bright red when ripe **Growth rate:** slow as a juvenile, medium thereafter **Climate:** 9a through 11 **Exposure:** part shade to full sun in

cooler Mediterranean climes **Soil:** humus laden and moist **Water needs:** medium to high **Salt tolerance:** none **Indoors:** good with very bright light, adequate air circulation, and humidity **Seed germination:** easy; within two months if fresh

Similar to Norfolk Island palm, Nikau palm is shorter, with a more bulbous crownshaft and longer leaves. It also is more tolerant of cold than Norfolk Island palm and less tolerant of hot climates.

## Roystonea oleracea
### South American royal palm, Venezuelan royal palm

**Distribution:** rain forest clearings and low mountainous tropical rain forest of the Lesser Antilles,

*Rhopalostylis sapida,* crownshaft. Paul Craft

*Roystonea oleracea,* in Florida.

*Roystonea oleracea*, in Venezuela. Paul Craft

Venezuela, and Colombia at elevations from sea level to 5280 ft. (1590 m) **Growth habit:** solitary **Height & width:** 100–150 ft. (30–45 m) tall, 20–30 ft. (6–9 m) wide **Trunk(s):** 80–130 ft. (24–39 m) tall, 2 ft. (60 cm) thick, light gray to white, swollen at the base and slightly tapering therefrom **Crownshaft:** 6 ft. (1.8 m) tall, only slightly tapering and scarcely thicker than the trunk, light to deep green, smooth **Leaves:** pinnate, 15 ft. (4.5 m) long, on 3-ft. (90-cm) long stout stalks, with many 3-ft. (90-cm) long narrow, pointed, dark green leaflets growing off the thick stalk at two different angles to create a slightly plumose effect, leaf crown hemispherical with about 20 leaves **Flower clusters:** large, whitish sprays of many branches emerging from great, upward-pointing, leathery horn-shaped bracts and bearing many small unisexual flowers of both sexes **Fruit:** round, less than ½ in. (12 mm) wide, purplish black when ripe **Growth rate:** fast once past the seedling stage **Climate:** 10 and 11, marginal in warmest parts of 9b **Exposure:** sun but part shade only when a seedling **Soil:** any but faster growing and better looking in humus-laden media; tolerates alkaline media **Water needs:** high **Salt tolerance:** little **Indoors:** not very good **Seed germination:** easy; three to four months if fresh and sown in warmth and moisture

No palm species is more majestic. Photographs seldom give a true sense of its grandeur, and an avenue with this species planted along it is an unbelievably grand sight.

## *Roystonea regia*
### Royal palm
**Distribution:** wet, swampy areas of the Caribbean coasts of Mexico, Belize, and Honduras, eastward through Cuba, the Bahamas, and the southern tip of Florida **Growth habit:** solitary **Height & width:** 80–100 ft. (24–30 m) tall, 20 ft. (6 m) wide **Trunk(s):** 60–100 ft. (18–30 m) tall, 18–20 in. (45–50 cm) thick, swollen at base, sometimes with a slight bulge near the middle, light gray to nearly pure white; younger parts of the stems and juvenile trees have prominent brown and widely spaced rings **Crownshaft:** 6

ft. (1.8 m) tall, dark green, cylindrical, smooth, slightly swollen at the base **Leaves:** pinnate, plumose, 12 ft. (4 m) long, with numerous 2- to 4-ft. (60- to 120-cm) long dark green pointed and fairly limp leaflets growing at different angles from the thick, stout 8-in. (20-cm) long stalks, leaf crown rounded with about 15 leaves **Flower clusters:** large, whitish sprays of many branches emerging from great, upward-pointing, leathery horn-shaped bracts and bearing many small unisexual flowers of both sexes **Fruit:** round, less than ½ in. (12 mm) wide, purplish black when ripe **Growth rate:** fast once past the seedling stage **Climate:** 10 and 11, marginal in warmest parts of 9b **Exposure:** full sun when older **Soil:**

*Roystonea regia*, in Florida.

any but relishes alkaline media **Water needs:** great **Salt tolerance:** slight; air only **Indoors:** good with much space, high humidity, and intense light **Seed germination:** easy; three to four months if fresh and sown in warmth and moisture

This is the most widely planted species in the genus, and with good reason. It is magnificently beautiful and is a veritable symbol of the wet tropics and the tropical look. It is hard to misplace this gorgeous palm in the landscape as it looks good even as a single specimen plant surrounded by space. Plantings of three or more individuals of varying heights are a vision of paradise itself, and its canopy-scape floating over lower vegetation is not only enthralling but also reminiscent of how it looked in much of its habitat, like the Everglades of southern Florida.

*Roystonea regia*, crownshaft, in Florida.

## Sabal causiarum
### Puerto Rican hat palm

**Distribution:** open sandy areas on Hispaniola **Growth habit:** solitary **Height & width:** 25–40 ft. (7.5–12 m) tall, 10–15 ft. (3–4.5 m) wide **Trunk(s):** 20–30 ft. (6–9 m) tall, 2 ft. (60 cm) thick, columnar and mostly smooth, slightly tapering from the base, light gray to nearly white **Crownshaft:** none **Leaves:** palmate, 6 ft. (1.8 m) wide or more, somewhat V-shaped in cross section, with deep green, wide, slightly limp segments extending halfway to the 5-ft. (1.5-m) long spineless stalk and having pendent ends **Flower clusters:** 10-ft. (3-m) long spikes with short branches extending beyond the rounded leaf crown and bearing small whitish bisexual flowers **Fruit:** pear-shaped; ½ in. (12 mm) long, black when ripe **Growth rate:** slow to medium **Climate:** 8b through 11, marginal in warm parts of 8a **Exposure:** sun **Soil:** any but relishes alkaline media **Water needs:** medium, but drought tolerant when established **Salt tolerance:** slight **Indoors:** good with intense light, adequate air circulation, and much space **Seed germination:** easy; within four months; needs a container at least 6 in. (15 cm) deep

This noble palm looks best in large groups or groves. It also is used to line walkways, promenades, and thoroughfares. It is great as a canopy-scape.

## Sabal domingensis
### Dominican palm

**Distribution:** hills and savannas of western Cuba and interior regions of Hispaniola **Growth habit:** solitary **Height & width:** 40–50 ft. (12–15 m) tall, 15–20 ft. (4.5–6 m) wide **Trunk(s):** 30–40 ft. (9–12 m) tall, 18–20 in. (45–50 cm) thick, smooth, light gray to tan, sometimes retaining many of the crisscrossing whitish leaf bases **Crownshaft:** none **Leaves:** palmate, 5–6 ft. (1.5–1.8 m) wide, divided into mostly stiff segments that protrude into the deep, dark green to deep bluish green blade and grow at slightly differing angles from the center of the blade, giving a three-dimensional aspect, on thick,

*Sabal causiarum*, in Florida.

*Sabal domingensis*, in the Dominican Republic. Paul Craft

heavy, spineless stalks 6–8 ft. (1.8–2.4 m) long **Flower clusters:** spikes 10 ft. (3 m) long with short branches extending beyond the rounded leaf crown and bearing small whitish bisexual flowers **Fruit:** round, ½ in. (12 mm) wide, black when ripe **Growth rate:** medium once past the seedling stage **Climate:** 9 through 11 **Exposure:** sun **Soil:** any but tolerates calcareous media **Water needs:** medium **Salt tolerance:** little **Indoors:** good with bright light and adequate air circulation **Seed germination:** easy; within four months; needs a container at least 6 in. (15 cm) deep

*Sabal domingensis* resembles *S. causiarum* but is even more appealing because of the larger, more open, rounded leaf crown and the darker colored leaves. It can be used as a specimen.

## Sabal mauritiiformis

**Distribution:** southern Mexico, eastern coastal Central America, Panama, and northern South America; a pocket of this species that seems to be indigenous has been discovered in northeastern Mexico by Richard S. Travis **Growth habit:** solitary **Height & width:** 50–80 ft. (15–24 m) tall, 10–15 ft. (3–4.5 m) wide **Trunk(s):** 40–80 ft. (12–24 m) tall, 10–12 in. (25–30 cm) thick, smooth and light tan to white **Crownshaft:** none **Leaves:** palmate, circular, 6 ft. (1.8 m) wide, deep green above, somewhat silvery beneath, on adult plants divided into long, limp segments with pendent ends, on juvenile plants even larger and divided into two or three very pleated wedge-shaped segments **Flower clusters:** spike 8 ft. (2.4 m) long with short branches usually extending just beyond the leaf crown and bearing small bisexual flowers **Fruit:** round to pear-shaped, ½ in. (12 mm) wide, black when ripe **Growth rate:** fast once past the seedling stage **Climate:** 10 and 11, marginal in warm parts of 9b **Exposure:** part shade when young, full sun when older **Soil:** any; relishes alkaline media but faster growing and better looking with humus **Water needs:** medium to high, but grows faster and looks better with copious amounts of water **Salt tolerance:** little **Indoors:**

*Sabal mauritiiformis*, in Florida.

difficult, thrives with good light for a while **Seed germination:** easy; within four months; needs a container at least 6 in. (15 cm) deep

Few palms are more beautiful. The species name tells a lot about its beauty, as *Mauritia flexuosa*, the plant after which it was named, is arguably the most beautiful palmate-leaved species in the Americas. The silhouette of this palm is galvanizing and makes an arresting canopy-scape. No palm is lovelier in groups of three or more individuals of varying heights.

## Sabal mexicana
### Texas palm, Mexican palmetto

**Distribution:** semiarid lowlands of southeastern Texas, through Mexico, and into Central America **Growth habit:** solitary **Height & width:** 40–60 ft. (12–18 m) tall, 10–12 ft. (3–4 m) wide **Trunk(s):** 40–50 ft. (12–15 m) tall, 1 ft. (30 cm) thick, the crisscrossing old leaf bases tending to remain attached especially in cultivation **Crownshaft:** none **Leaves:** palmate, 5–6 ft. (1.5–1.8 m) wide, divided into narrow, stiff segments that intrude deeply into the deep green leaf blade creating a somewhat V-shaped appearance, on spineless stalks 3–4 ft. (90–120 cm) long **Flower clusters:** spikes 4–6 ft. (1.2–1.8 m) long with short branches partially hidden in the crown and bearing small bisexual flowers, often blooming when quite young **Fruit:** round, ½ in. (12 mm) wide, black when ripe **Growth rate:** slow **Climate:** 8b through 11 **Exposure:** part shade when young; full sun when older **Soil:** any including calcareous media **Water needs:** low, but grows faster with regular irrigation **Salt tolerance:** some; slight soil salinity **Indoors:** difficult **Seed germination:** easy; within four months; needs a container at least 6 in. (15 cm) deep

While visually similar to *Sabal palmetto*, *S. mexicana* is more robust looking and has a larger, usually more globular leaf crown and larger, more attractive leaf bases. It makes an excellent focal point in larger gardens.

## Sabal minor
### Dwarf palmetto, bush palmetto

**Distribution:** an understory plant of the southeastern United States, west to eastern and central Texas, southern Oklahoma, southern Arkansas, and northeastern Mexico **Growth habit:** solitary **Height & width:** 6–20 ft. (1.8–6

*Sabal mexicana*, in Florida. Paul Craft

*Sabal minor*, in habitat in Texas.

m) tall, 8–10 ft. (2.4–3 m) wide **Trunk(s):** usually underground, but aboveground trunks seen in swamps of southern Louisiana and eastern Texas **Crownshaft:** none **Leaves:** palmate, 4–6 ft. (1.2–1.8 m) wide, with stiff dark green segments usually in two groups **Flower clusters:** narrow spikes of branches exceeding the leaf crown and bearing small white fragrant bisexual flowers **Fruit:** round, ¼ in. (6 mm) wide, shiny black when ripe **Growth rate:** very slow **Climate:** 6 through 11, marginal in warmest parts of 5b **Exposure:** shade to part shade **Soil:** moist, humus laden, even mucky **Water needs:** high **Salt tolerance:** none **Indoors:** unknown but should be easy with enough water and bright light **Seed germination:** easy; within four months; needs a container at least 6 in. (15 cm) deep

The species is as beautiful as any purely tropical palm when used as a giant groundcover under canopy, but it is out of place as a specimen plant surrounded by space and in full sun. It is outstanding in low, swampy areas, where it gives a tropical look to decidedly nontropical regions.

## *Sabal palmetto*
### Palmetto, cabbage palm

**Distribution:** from Cape Fear, North Carolina, south through peninsular Florida, the Bahamas, and Cuba **Growth habit:** solitary **Height & width:** 60–90 ft. (18–27 m) tall, 12 ft. (4 m) wide **Trunk(s):** 50–80 ft. (15–24 m) tall, 10–12 in. (25–30 cm) thick, light tan to nearly white; younger trees and younger parts of older trees often covered in crisscrossing light-colored old leaf bases; very old specimens almost never have them **Crownshaft:** none **Leaves:** palmate, 4–6 ft. (1.2–1.8 m) wide, divided into segments that intrude deeply into the blade, on spineless stalks 5–6 ft. (1.5–1.8 m) long **Flower clusters:** spikes 8 ft. (2.4 m) long with short branches bearing small bisexual flowers **Fruit:** round, ½ in. (12 mm)

*Sabal minor*, in Florida. Paul Craft

*Sabal palmetto*, in Florida.

wide, black when ripe **Growth rate:** very slow as a seedling, medium slow after trunk formation **Climate:** 8 through 11, marginal in warmest parts of 7b **Exposure:** part shade when young, full sun when older **Soil:** any but faster growing and better looking with moist, humus-laden media **Water needs:** medium, but grows faster with regular irrigation **Salt tolerance:** medium; great salinity slowly kills it **Indoors:** not very good **Seed germination:** easy; within four months; needs a container at least 6 in. (15 cm) deep

The species is of incredible beauty as a specimen or in small groups. If planted in rows along highways like lines of utility poles, it looks truly abominable, especially when its naturally globular crowns are constantly pruned.

## Sabal uresana
### Blue palmetto

**Distribution:** northwestern Mexico in the states of Chihuahua and Sonora, in the foothills of the Sierra Madre Occidental in dry subtropical thorn forests from sea level to an elevation of 4500 ft. (1350 m) **Growth habit:** solitary **Height & width:** 40–60 ft. (12–18 m) tall, 10–15 ft. (3–4.5 m) wide **Trunk(s):** 40–60 ft. (12–18 m) tall, 18 in. (45 cm) thick **Crownshaft:** none **Leaves:** palmate, 3–4 ft. (90–120 cm) long, divided into segments that protrude deeply into the bluish green to silvery blue blade, on spineless stalks 6–8 ft. (1.8–2.4 m) long **Flower clusters:** spikes 10 ft. (3 m) long with short branches bearing whitish bisexual flowers **Fruit:** ovoid, ¼ in. (6 mm) long, black when ripe **Growth rate:** slow **Climate:** 9a through 11 and dry, warm parts of 8a **Exposure:** full sun **Soil:** any but relishes alkaline media **Water needs:** low **Salt tolerance:** slight **Indoors:** unknown **Seed germination:** easy; within four months; needs a container at least 6 in. (15 cm) deep

*Sabal uresana*, in Florida.

Some specimens have true silvery blue leaves and are locally referred to as *la palma blanca*, "the white palm." These individuals are much sought after and are eminently worth the trouble.

## Satakentia liukiuensis

**Distribution:** wet forests of the Ryukyu Archipelago of Japan **Growth habit:** solitary **Height & width:** 40–50 ft. (12–15 m) tall, 15–20 ft. (4.5–6 m) wide **Trunk(s):** 30–50 ft. (9–15 m) tall, 1 ft. (30 cm) thick, tan to light gray and mostly smooth, with dark brown rings **Crownshaft:** 2–3 ft. (60–90 cm) tall, dark olive green, reddish brown, or purplish brown, cylindrical, slightly bulging at the base **Leaves:** pinnate, 8–10 ft. (2.4–3 m) long on a short spineless stalk, many regularly spaced, deep green, limp, narrow leaflets, mostly in a flat plane, midrib usually twisted so that leaflets at the outer half are vertically oriented, creating an especially beautiful silhouette, leaf crown globular with 12 to 14 spreading leaves **Flower clusters:** broomlike sprays of stiff, thick whitish branches bearing unisexual flowers of both sexes **Fruit:** oblong, ½ in. (12 mm) wide, black when ripe **Growth rate:** medium to fast **Climate:** 10b and 11, marginal in

*Satakentia liukiuensis*, crownshaft and stem, in Florida.

*Satakentia liukiuensis*, in Florida. Chuck Hubbuch

*Schippia concolor*, in Florida.

warm parts of 10a **Exposure:** part shade to full sun **Soil:** humus laden and moist; tolerates calcareous media if there is humus or a thick mulch **Water needs:** medium to high, but grows faster and looks better with regular irrigation **Salt tolerance:** slight **Indoors:** good with intense light and adequate air circulation **Seed germination:** easy; within six months; slightly unripe seeds seem to germinate better than fully ripe ones

The crown and leaves look much like those of a coconut palm, giving this species the same landscaping uses. While still not common in cultivation, the species is rapidly gaining acceptance in southern Florida where it seems to do exceptionally well.

## *Schippia concolor*

**Distribution:** rain forest and wet pinelands of Belize, to 1575 ft. (480 m) elevation **Growth**

**habit:** solitary **Height & width:** 20–35 ft. (6–10.5 m) tall, 6–10 ft. (1.8–3 m) wide **Trunk(s):** 20–30 ft. (6–9 m) tall, 4 in. (10 cm) thick, upper parts covered with dark brown fibers and a few leaf base remnants, lower parts smooth and light gray **Crownshaft:** none **Leaves:** palmate, nearly circular, divided into 16 to 18 narrow, pointed segments that extend two thirds into the blade, which is dark green above, slightly paler beneath, on thin, spineless stalks 6 ft. (1.8 m) long **Flower clusters:** sprays 2 ft. (60 cm) long with short greenish branches bearing white bisexual flowers **Fruit:** round, 1 in. (2.5 cm) wide, soft and white or nearly so when ripe **Growth rate:** fairly slow **Climate:** 10 and 11, marginal in warmest parts of 9b **Exposure:** part shade to sun **Soil:** any; adapts well to alkaline media but faster growing and better looking with moist, humus-laden media **Water needs:** medium,

*Serenoa repens*, leaf.

*Schippia concolor*, fruit, in Florida.

but does best with regular irrigation **Salt toler-ance:** none **Indoors:** good with very bright light and excellent air circulation **Seed germination:** fairly easy; within four months

The airy leaf crown of exquisitely elegant proportions creates a lovely silhouette. The tree does not look good as an isolated specimen surrounded by space but is more than charming as a small canopy-scape or against a highly contrasting background so that its form can be easily seen.

## *Serenoa repens*
### Saw palmetto, silver saw palmetto

**Distribution:** southeastern Louisiana, southern Mississippi, southern Alabama, most of Florida, southern and coastal Georgia, and southern South Carolina **Growth habit:** clustering **Height & width:** 6–30 ft. (1.8–9 m) tall, 12 ft. (4 m) wide **Trunk(s):** subterranean until of some age, with very old stems reaching 18 ft. (5.4 m) or more, covered in fibers and leaf bases **Crownshaft:** none **Leaves:** palmate, semicircular to nearly circular, 3 ft. (90 cm) wide, divided into many pointed stiff segments that extend two thirds into the blade and vary from light to deep green to silvery green to pure silvery blue, on stalks 3–5 ft. (90–150 cm) long with tiny backward-pointing spines **Flower clusters:** spikes of short branches bearing white bisexual flowers **Fruit:** ellipsoid, ½–1 in. (12–25 mm) wide, shiny blue to black when ripe **Growth rate:** slow, especially before forming an aboveground stem **Climate:** 8 through 11, marginal in 7b **Exposure:** part shade to full sun **Soil:** any medium that is not waterlogged for extended periods **Water needs:** low, but adapts to very moist conditions **Salt tolerance:** high **Indoors:** only with extraordinary amounts of light and air circulation **Seed germination:** easy; within four months; needs a container at least 6 in. (15 cm) deep

*Serenoa repens*, at Lake June, Florida.

The forms with silvery blue or blue-green leaves are usually considered more attractive than the plain green forms, but all make a dramatic, tropical-looking accent in the landscape. Great masses of the plants are tiresome to contemplate, however, even in nature. None of the colors seems attractive when isolated with surrounding space, and the great clumps look much better when integrated into a shrub border or mixed with tall but not overly umbrageous trees. This palm is nearly impossible to transplant if not containerized, so site it carefully.

## Syagrus coronata

**Distribution:** eastern Brazil in seasonally dry places **Growth habit:** solitary **Height & width:** 30–50 ft. (9–15 m) tall, 12–18 ft. (4–5.4 m) wide **Trunk(s):** 30–40 ft. (9–12 m) tall, 1 ft. (30 cm)

thick, uppermost part always covered with old leaf bases, which create a squared and angular effect **Crownshaft:** none **Leaves:** pinnate, plumose, dark green above and silvery green beneath **Flower clusters:** 3-ft. (90-cm) long yellowish branches emerging from tough woody bracts and bearing white unisexual flowers of both sexes **Fruit:** oval, 1–1½ in. (2.5–4 cm) long, orange when ripe **Growth rate:** slow as a seedling; medium after trunk formation; faster in optimum growing conditions **Climate:** 10 and 11, marginal in 9b **Exposure:** sun **Soil:** any; relishes alkaline media but faster growing and better looking in moist, humus-laden media **Water needs:** medium **Salt tolerance:** slight **Indoors:** only with much light, space, and very good air circulation **Seed germination:** easy; within three months if fresh

*Syagrus coronata*, flowers in bracts, in Australia.
Paul Craft

*Syagrus coronata*, in Florida.

This palm is beautiful even as an isolated specimen surrounded by space but looks better in groups of three or more individuals of varying heights; a grove is glorious. Because of the almost unique pattern of leaf bases and scars on its trunk, it is also architectural in aspect and provides unending pleasure in the up-close contemplation of its stem. It makes a wonderful large tub plant.

## Syagrus romanzoffiana
### Queen palm
**Distribution:** forests in southeastern Brazil and adjacent parts of Argentina, Paraguay, and Uruguay **Growth habit:** solitary **Height & width:** 45–90 ft. (13.5–27 m) tall, 10–15 ft. (3–4.5 m) wide **Trunk(s):** 40–75 ft. (12–22.5 m) tall, 10–20 in. (25–50 cm) thick, upper parts often green with widely spaced rings, lower parts light gray to white and almost smooth **Crownshaft:** none **Leaves:** pinnate, plumose, 8–15 ft. (2.4–4.5 m) long, with many medium to dark green, usually limp leaflets 1–2 ft. (30–60 cm) long **Flower clusters:** many yellow pendent 2- to 5-ft. (60- to 150-cm) long branches emerging from very large woody boat-shaped bracts and bearing white unisexual flowers of both sexes **Fruit:** ovoid, 1 in. (2.5 cm) long, light to deep orange, occasionally yellow, when ripe **Growth rate:** fast; very fast with optimum growing conditions **Climate:** 9b through 11 depending on provenance, with some specimens adapting to 9a and even the warmest parts of 8b **Exposure:** sun **Soil:** humus laden; not adapted to calcareous media without amendments **Water needs:** high **Salt tolerance:** almost none **Indoors:** only with very in-

*Syagrus romanzoffiana.*

*Syagrus schizophylla*, in Florida.

tense light and good air circulation **Seed germination:** easy; within three months if fresh

This species is among the most beautiful, tropical-looking palms that can be grown outside of tropical areas. It looks enough like the royal palm (*Roystonea*) that it can be used to line streets and avenues. Its canopy-scape is thrilling, and a specimen group of individuals of varying heights is among the most picturesque landscaping tableaux. In 2003 a lethal disease attacked adult trees in southern Florida. This quick-acting, windborne malady is probably fungal in nature and has no known cure.

## Syagrus schizophylla
### Arikury palm

**Distribution:** sandy coastal forests of eastern Brazil **Growth habit:** mostly solitary, occasionally clustering **Height & width:** 15–25 ft. (4.5–7.5 m) tall, 8–12 ft. (2.4–4 m) wide **Trunk(s):** 8–15 ft. (2.4–4.5 m) tall, 10 in. (25 cm) thick with the narrow, wickerlike old leaf bases, only 6 in. (15 cm) thick without **Crownshaft:** none

**Leaves:** pinnate, 6 ft. (1.8-m) long, on spiny stalks 2 ft. (60 cm) long, with many narrow olive to dark green 1-ft. (30-cm) long leaflets that are stiff in young leaves but mostly pendent in older ones, leaf crown hemispherical **Flower clusters:** sprays 2 ft. (60 cm) long with yellowish branches bearing white unisexual flowers of both sexes **Fruit:** egg-shaped; 1 in. (2.5 cm) long, red when ripe, edible **Growth rate:** slow as a seedling, medium slow after trunk formation **Climate:** 10 and 11, marginal in warmest parts of 9b **Exposure:** part shade or sun **Soil:** humus laden but readily adapts to poorer media if moisture is provided **Water needs:** high **Salt tolerance:** none **Indoors:** good **Seed germination:** easy; within three months if fresh

This architectural-looking species is best in up-close and intimate sites; it is the perfect patio palm. Its beauty is ruined if the tree is planted as a single specimen surrounded by space unless it is incorporated into lower vegetation above which its beautiful silhouette may be enjoyed. It does look much better as a specimen if planted in groups of

*Syagrus schizophylla*, trunk, in Florida.

*Syagrus schizophylla*, fruit, in Florida.

three or more individuals of varying heights, but its small stature seems to mitigate against this. If one is fortunate enough to have a clustering individual, almost any site is a good one. Arikury palm is slightly prone to lethal yellowing.

## *Thrinax excelsa*
### Jamaican thatch palm

**Distribution:** hills and low mountains of extreme eastern Jamaica **Growth habit:** solitary **Height & width:** 40–55 ft. (12–16.5 m) tall, 10–18 ft. (3–5.4 m) wide **Trunk(s):** 25–35 ft. (7.5–10.5 m) tall, 8 in. (20 cm) thick, light gray with closely set rings or grooves **Crownshaft:** none **Leaves:** palmate, circular, 5–6 ft. (1.5–1.8 m) wide, divided into limp segments that extend two-thirds into the blade and have pendent tips, deep green above, slightly grayish green beneath, on thin, unarmed stalks 5 ft. (1.5 m) long **Flower clusters:** pendent sprays 3–4 ft. (90–120 cm) long with many short yellowish branches bearing white bisexual flowers **Fruit:** round, ½ in. (12 mm) wide, white, in pendent

*Thrinax excelsa*, in Florida.

*Thrinax excelsa*, fruit.

*Thrinax morrisii*, flowers, in Florida.

masses **Growth rate:** medium slow **Climate:** 10 and 11 **Exposure:** part shade when young; full sun when older **Soil:** any including alkaline media **Water needs:** low to medium but grows faster in moist media **Salt tolerance:** moderate **Indoors:** only with bright light and very good air circulation **Seed germination:** fairly easy; within three months if fresh; needs a container at least 6 in. (15 cm) deep

Because of its large leaves, Jamaican thatch palm is the most lush and most tropical-looking species in the genus. It is beautiful and choice as a younger plant and is captivating up close and in an intimate site. When older it is beautiful as a specimen, especially in groups of three or more individuals of varying heights. In truth, it is hard to misplace.

## Thrinax morrisii
### Key thatch palm, silver thatch palm

**Distribution:** open and low forests of the Florida Keys, the Bahamas, western Cuba, the western tip of Haiti, and Puerto Rico **Growth habit:** solitary **Height & width:** 20–35 ft. (6–10.5 m) tall, 8–12 ft. (2.4–4 m) wide **Trunk(s):** 25–35 ft. (7.5–10.5 m) tall, 8 in. (20 cm) thick, light gray to nearly white with closely set rings or grooves **Crownshaft:** none **Leaves:** palmate, semicircular in young plants, circular in older ones, 2–3 ft. (60–90 cm) wide, divided into lance-shaped segments that extend almost to the center of the blade, deep green above, silvery green or silver beneath, on thin stalks 3–5 ft. (90–150 cm) long **Flower clusters:** 3- to 5-ft. (90- to 150-cm) long pendent yellowish branches bearing white bisexual flow-

*Thrinax morrisii*, in Florida.

ers **Fruit:** round, ½ in. (12 mm) wide, white, in pendent masses **Growth rate:** slow **Climate:** 9b through 11 **Exposure:** sun **Soil:** any but relishes alkaline media **Water needs:** low, but grows faster and looks better with regular irrigation **Salt tolerance:** high **Indoors:** only with intense light and very good air circulation **Seed germination:** fairly easy; within three months if fresh; needs a container at least 6 in. (15 cm) deep

The rounded, airy crown is beautiful as a canopy-scape, but the palm is equally satisfactory in an intimate site where its little starburst-shaped leaves dance in a breeze.

### Thrinax radiata
Florida thatch palm

**Distribution:** coasts of the Florida Keys, the Bahamas, western Cuba, Puerto Rico, Hispaniola Yucatán, and Belize **Growth habit:** almost always solitary, rarely suckering **Height & width:** 30–50 ft. (9–15 m) tall, 6–9 ft. (1.8–2.7 m) wide **Trunk(s):** 30–40 ft. (9–12 m) tall, 5 in. (13 cm)

*Thrinax radiata*, leaning over water, in Florida.

*Thrinax radiata*, upright-growing, in Florida.

*Trachycarpus fortunei*, in California. Paul Craft

thick, white and mostly smooth **Crownshaft:** none **Leaves:** palmate, circular, 3 ft. (90 cm) wide, divided into segments that extend two-thirds into the blade and have pendent tips, deep green above, silvery green beneath, on thin stalks 3 ft. (90 cm) long **Flower clusters:** sprays 3–4 ft. (90–120 cm) long with many short yellowish branches bearing white bisexual flowers **Fruit:** round, ½ in. (12 mm) wide, white when ripe **Growth rate:** very slow **Climate:** 10 and 11, marginal in warm parts of 9b **Exposure:** full sun, slower growing in part shade **Soil:** any fast-draining medium **Water needs:** low **Salt tolerance:** complete **Indoors:** not good **Seed germination:** fairly easy; within three months if fresh; needs a container at least 6 in. (15 cm) deep

Florida thatch palm is a perfect candidate for the beach as well as sunny inland areas. Its crown is open and airy when young or when planted in partial shade but is tightly globular and dense when older and in full sun—so much so that the leaves are usually obscured, making it a distinctive and picturesque canopy-scape.

## *Trachycarpus fortunei*
### Windmill palm, Chinese windmill palm, chusan palm

**Distribution:** probably eastern and central China **Growth habit:** solitary **Height & width:** 25–50 ft. (7.5–15 m) tall, 8–10 ft. (2.4–3 m) wide **Trunk(s):** 30–40 ft. (9–12 m) tall, 8–10 in. (20–25 cm) thick but usually appearing much thicker because of adherent leaf bases and associated fibers **Crownshaft:** none **Leaves:** palmate, semicircular to nearly circular, 3 ft. (90 cm) wide, divided into many lance-shaped, pointed leathery deep green segments that mostly intrude deeply into the blade, on stalks 3 ft. (90 cm) long **Flower clusters:** many short, congested yellow branches bearing yellow unisexual and/or bisexual flowers **Fruit:** oblong to kidney-shaped, ½ in. (12 mm) wide, purplish when ripe **Growth rate:** medium, but grows faster in optimum conditions **Climate:** 7b through 11, marginal in 7a **Exposure:** part shade to full sun except in hot tropical climates where it is nearly impossible **Soil:** widely adaptable but best with organic

*Trachycarpus wagnerianus*, in California. Richard Travis

material **Water needs:** moderate **Salt tolerance:** very little **Indoors:** good in cool but frostless enclosures **Seed germination:** easy; within three months if fresh; needs a container at least 6 in. (15 cm) deep

A second form of windmill palm, once known as the separate species *Trachycarpus wagnerianus*, seems to have originated in Japan and is generally smaller than the typical windmill in all its parts. The leaves especially are not only smaller but also much stiffer and sometimes rather cup-shaped. The "wagnerianus" form is much more tolerant of wind and similar physical abuse and is usually considered more choice and beautiful than the typical windmill. Both forms of this palm have a beautiful silhouette and make wonderful canopy-scapes. The "wagnerianus" form is especially suited to more intimate settings. The typical and older known windmill should not be planted where its crown is regularly subjected to high winds. It looks nice planted alone and surrounded by space but is even more satisfying in groups of three or more individuals of varying heights. Windmill palm is slightly prone to lethal yellowing.

*Trachycarpus martianunus*, in California. Richard Travis

## *Trachycarpus martianunus*

**Distribution:** mountainous rain forests of northeastern India, Nepal, and northern Myanmar (Burma) at elevations from 5000 to 8000 ft. (1500–2400 m) **Growth habit:** solitary **Height & width:** 15–25 ft. (4.5–7.5 m) tall, 8–12 ft. (2.4–4 m) wide **Trunk(s):** 15–20 ft. (4.5–6 m) tall, 7 in. (18 cm) thick, gray to nearly white without leaf bases or fibers **Crownshaft:** none **Leaves:** palmate, circular on young plants, semicircular on older ones, 3–4 ft. (90–120 cm) wide, divided into many narrow, stiff segments that extend halfway into the blade, deep green above and grayish beneath, on stalks 4 ft. (1.2 m) long, new growth and stalks covered in white felt **Flower clusters:** many short, congested yellow branches bearing yellow unisexual and/or bisexual flowers **Fruit:** ovoid, ½ in. (12 mm) long, bluish black when ripe **Growth rate:** medium to slow **Climate:** 8 through 11 in

tropical to subtropical conditions but not adaptable to hot, dry climes **Exposure:** part shade when young, otherwise full sun **Soil:** moist and humus laden **Water needs:** medium to high **Salt tolerance:** none **Indoors:** unknown **Seed germination:** easy; within three months if fresh; needs a container at least 6 in. (15 cm) deep

Because of its open crown and stiff leaf segments, this palm is dramatically beautiful, especially in silhouette.

## *Trithrinax brasiliensis*
### Brazilian needle palm

**Distribution:** inland open and dry savannas of extreme southeastern Brazil **Growth habit:** mostly solitary, sometimes clustering **Height**

& width: 35–50 ft. (10.5–15 m) tall, 8–12 ft. (2.4–4 m) wide **Trunk(s):** 30–50 ft. (9–15 m) tall, 10 in. (25 cm) thick but looking much thicker because of the mass of fibers and needlelike projections from old leaf bases; sometimes found with a "skirt" of dead leaves in nature **Crownshaft:** none **Leaves:** palmate, semicircular, 3–4 ft. (90–120 cm) wide, divided into many narrow, stiff, pointed segments that extend at least halfway to the blade, light to dark green to bluish or silvery green, on stalks 2 ft. (60 cm) long **Flower clusters:** 2- to 3-ft. (60- to 90-cm) long congested yellow branches bearing white bisexual flowers **Fruit:** round, ½ in. (12 mm) wide, yellowish brown when ripe, in pendent tight masses **Growth rate:** slow **Climate:** 8 through 11 in dry climes, 9 through 11 in wet climes **Exposure:** sun **Soil:** any well-drained medium including alkaline ones **Water needs:** low **Salt tolerance:** medium **Indoors:** only in a nonhumid space with bright light **Seed germination:** easy; within three months if fresh; needs a container at least 6 in. (15 cm) deep

The attraction of this species is its picturesque trunk, so pruning off the fiber mat and its accompanying spines leaves a characterless stem. One might as well plant a windmill palm (*Trachycarpus fortunei*), which grows faster and looks like this species minus its trunk covering. Removing the old, dead bottom parts of the petioles can be effective, however. Because of its slow growth rate, this palm serves well for years as a close-up specimen. It is especially nice combined with rocks, cactus, or succulents. Old clustering individuals make beautiful specimens, even when surrounded by space.

## Trithrinax campestris

**Distribution:** semiarid open savannas of northern Argentina and west central Uruguay **Growth habit:** clustering **Height & width:** 20–35 ft. (6–10.5 m) tall, 6–9 ft. (1.8–2.7 m) wide **Trunk(s):** 15–25 ft. (4.5–7.5 m) tall, 12–18 in. (30–45 cm) thick, covered in a thick "skirt" of dead leaves beneath which the upper parts are covered in an intricate reticulated network

*Trithrinax brasiliensis*, in California.

of tightly woven black fibers and downward-pointing spines **Crownshaft:** none **Leaves:** palmate, diamond- or wedge-shaped, 2–2½ ft. (60–75 cm) wide, deeply divided into very stiff segments with needlelike tips, silvery to bluish green to silvery blue above, a glaucous yellow-green beneath, on stalks 2 ft. (60 cm) long **Flower clusters:** pendent spikes 1–2 ft. (30–60 cm) long with congested yellow branches bearing tiny white bisexual flowers **Fruit:** round, ½ in. (12 mm) wide, brown when ripe **Growth rate:** slow to very slow **Climate:** 7 through 11 in dry climes, 8 through 11 in wet climates **Exposure:** sun **Soil:** any well-drained medium that is neither too acidic nor too alkaline **Water**

*Trithrinax campestris*, a juvenile tree, in California. Richard Travis

*Trithrinax campestris*, a mature tree, in habitat in Argentina. Gaston Torres-Vera

needs: low **Salt tolerance:** medium **Indoors:** not good **Seed germination:** easy; within three months if fresh; needs a container at least 6 in. (15 cm) deep

No palm is more picturesque. Old clustering individuals are stunningly attractive even as specimens surrounded by space, and from a distance, look like small silvery washingtonias. It is hard to overpraise this palm. Beware of the steel-like rigid leaflets, which can be as dangerous as knives.

## *Veitchia arecina*
### Montgomery palm, sunshine palm

**Distribution:** low mountainous rain forests of Vanuatu **Growth habit:** solitary **Height & width:** 60–90 ft. (18–27 m) tall, 15–20 ft. (4.5–6 m) wide **Trunk(s):** 50–80 ft. (15–24 m) tall, 1 ft. (30 cm) thick above the swollen base **Crownshaft:** 4–5 ft. (1.2–1.5 m) tall, slightly thicker than the trunk, shiny silvery green, somewhat bulging at the base **Leaves:** pinnate, slightly ascending, gently arched, 8–12 ft. (2.4–4 m)

*Veitchia arecina*, in Florida.

*Veitchia joannis*, in Florida.

long, with many very deep green 3-ft. (90-cm) long lance-shaped slightly pendent leaflets, leaf crown hemispherical and somewhat sparse **Flower clusters:** sprays 3–4 ft. (90–120 cm) in diameter with thick, succulent waxy branches bearing greenish white unisexual flowers of both sexes **Fruit:** ovoid to elliptical, 1½ in. (4 cm) long, bright red when ripe, in large pendent clusters **Growth rate:** medium when very young; fast in middle age; slow when old **Climate:** 10b and 11 **Exposure:** part shade when young, otherwise full sun **Soil:** any fast-draining medium including alkaline ones **Water needs:** medium to high **Salt tolerance:** slight **Indoors:** only with much space, bright light, and very good air circulation **Seed germination:** easy and fast; within a month if fresh

Not many palm species look good planted anywhere, but this one does. It is difficult to find words to describe its beauty as a canopy-scape, especially in groups of three or more individuals of varying heights; its silhouette is simply astonishing. The tree is slightly prone to lethal yellowing.

## *Veitchia joannis*
### Joannis palm

**Distribution:** low mountainous rain forest of Fiji **Growth habit:** solitary **Height & width:** 80–120 ft. (24–36 m) tall, 15–20 ft. (4.5–6 m) wide **Trunk(s):** 70–110 ft. (21–33 m) tall, 12–16 in. (30–40 cm) thick above the swollen base, very light gray to white **Crownshaft:** 4–6 ft. (1.2–1.8 m) tall, as thick as the trunk, yellow-green to olive green, slightly bulged at the base **Leaves:** pinnate, ascending and gently arching, 10–12 ft. (3–4 m) long, with many 3-ft. (90-cm) long, wide, ridged, deep green, lance-shaped leaflets that hang from the midrib in a vertical curtain, leaf crown nearly spherical **Flower clusters:** sprays similar to those of *Veitchia arecina* but smaller, with thick, succulent waxy branches bearing greenish white unisexual flowers of both sexes **Fruit:** egg-shaped to conical, 1½–2 in. (4–5 cm) long, deep orange to bright red when ripe **Growth rate:** quite fast, especially once past the juvenile stage **Climate:** 10b and 11 **Exposure:** full sun **Soil:** any moist medium that is neither too acidic nor too alkaline

**Water needs:** high **Salt tolerance:** none **Indoors:** only with an extraordinarily large space and bright light **Seed germination:** easy and fast; within a month if fresh

This species is among the few rivals of the coconut palm for absolute beauty and grace.

### Verschaffeltia splendida
Seychelles stilt palm

**Distribution:** mountainous rain forest of the Seychelles **Growth habit:** solitary **Height & width:** 50–70 ft. (15–21 m) tall, 12–18 ft. (4–5.4 m) wide **Trunk(s):** 20–40 ft. (16–12 m) tall, 8 in. (20 cm) thick above a narrow 4- to 6-ft. (1.2- to 1.8-m) tall cone of stilt roots, upper parts covered in sharp black downward-pointing spines **Crownshaft:** 2–3 ft. (60–90 cm) tall, usually light green, slightly bulging at the base **Leaves:** pinnate, 5–8 ft.

*Verschaffeltia splendida*, leaf of a young tree, in Florida.

*Verschaffeltia splendida*, in Australia. Paul Craft      *Verschaffeltia splendida*, spiny trunk, in Florida.

(1.5–2.4 m) long, entire and elliptical with a notch at the end when younger, older leaves on larger plants grown outdoors are invariably divided by wind into variously shaped segments of varying number **Flower clusters:** 4–6 ft. (1.2–1.8 m) long with several thin greenish yellow branches bearing small yellow unisexual flowers of both sexes **Fruit:** round, 1 in. (2.5 cm) wide, brown, in pendent masses **Growth rate:** medium to slow **Climate:** 10b and 11 **Exposure:** part shade to full sun **Soil:** humus laden **Water needs:** high **Salt tolerance:** none **Indoors:** only as a juvenile **Seed germination:** easy; within a month if fresh and sown in warmth and moisture

Seychelles stilt palm is among the world's most beautiful palm species. Its large leaves, even when segmented by wind, are indescribably lovely, and its overall form is perfect. It looks nice as a specimen plant, even with only one individual, but is simply stunning in groups of three individuals of varying heights and ages. This palm seems to cry out for an intimate site where its beauty can be contemplated up close, but its ultimate size prevents such placement; when young, however, it is perfection seen up close.

## Washingtonia filifera
### California fan palm, cotton palm (England)

**Distribution:** in arroyos and canyons and near natural springs in southern interior California, extreme western Arizona, and Baja California **Growth habit:** solitary **Height & width:** 50–70 ft. (15–21 m) tall, 10–16 ft. (3–4.8 m) wide **Trunk(s):** 40–60 ft. (12–18 m) tall, 3–4 ft. (90–120 cm) thick but often appearing much thicker because of a "skirt" of dead leaves **Crownshaft:** none **Leaves:** palmate, hemispherical to nearly circular, 6–8 ft. (1.8–2.4 m) wide, with many lance-shaped segments that extend more than halfway to the blade, deep to light grayish green, with pendant tips and with long curling white threads between the segments, on thick stalks 6 ft. (1.8 m) long with wicked 1- to 2-in. (2.5- to 5-cm) long slightly recurved spines that often have a reddish tint **Flower clusters:** very long spikes of yellowish white branches curving out

of the leaf crown and bearing small white unisexual flowers **Fruit:** round, ¼ in. (6 mm) wide, dark brown to black when ripe **Growth rate:** slow as a seedling, medium thereafter **Climate:** 7 through 11 in dry climes, 8 through 11 in wet, humid climes **Exposure:** sun **Soil:** any well-drained medium including alkaline ones **Water needs:** low, but grows faster and looks better with regular irrigation **Salt tolerance:** medium **Indoors:** not very good **Seed germination:** easy; within a month if fresh; needs a container at least 6 in. (15 cm) deep

The trunks of older palms are not attractive up close, and the trees look better when lining avenues or as canopy-scapes, where their wonderful crown silhouettes accent the horizon. Specimen groups of individuals of varying heights are extremely attractive and tropical looking as well.

*Washingtonia filifera*, in California. Paul Craft

## *Washingtonia robusta*
## Mexican fan palm

**Distribution:** in arroyos and canyons and at natural springs in Baja California and Sonora, Mexico **Growth habit:** solitary **Height & width:** 70–100 ft. (21–30 m) tall, 8–12 ft. (2.4–4 m) wide **Trunk(s):** 70–90 ft. (21–27 m) tall, 12–18 in. (30–45 cm) thick, sometimes covered in the "skirt" of dead leaf bases, otherwise older parts are very light gray to almost white **Crownshaft:** none **Leaves:** palmate, semicircular to almost circular, 3–4 ft. (90–120 cm) wide, divided into segments that extend more than halfway into the deep green blade and have pendent tips, on stalks 4 ft. (1.2 m) long and armed with reddish-tinged slightly recurved spines 1–2 in. (2.5–5 cm) long **Flower clusters:** spikes of yellowish white branches shorter than those of *Washington filifera* and bearing small white bisexual flowers **Fruit:** round, ¼ in. (6 mm) wide, dark brown to black when ripe **Growth rate:** fast to quite fast once past the seedling stage **Climate:** 9b through 11, marginal in 9a **Exposure:** sun **Soil:** any including alkaline media **Water needs:** medium but grows faster with regular irrigation **Salt tolerance:** medium **Indoors:** only in very large and bright atriums **Seed germination:** easy; within a month if fresh; needs a container at least 6 in. (15 cm) deep

Mexican fan palm is by far the most commonly planted palm species in Southern California, far southern Texas, and Phoenix and Tucson in Arizona. It needs lots of space. Any of the plants currently sold are of hybrid origin. Better known as "filibustas," they often look close to the pure species but are hardier to cold, especially wet cold.

*Washingtonia robusta.*

## Wodyetia bifurcata
### Foxtail palm

**Distribution:** sandy soils in rocky scrubland of Cape York in Queensland, Australia **Growth habit:** solitary **Height & width:** 40–60 ft. (12–18 m) tall, 10–12 ft. (3–4 m) wide **Trunk(s):** 30–50 ft. (9–15 m) tall, 12–18 in. (30–45 cm) thick at the base, in old plants tapering to 8 in. (20 cm) at the beginning of the crownshaft **Crownshaft:** mainly 3 ft. (90 cm) tall, bluish green, smooth, continued tapering of the trunk below **Leaves:** pinnate, plumose, 8–10 ft. (2.4–3 m) long, with many dark green to deep bluish green, narrowly wedge-shaped leaflets with jagged ends, on short dark stalks 6–10 in. (15–25 cm) long, leaf crown usually globular **Flower clusters:** much-branched spikes 2–3 ft. (60–90 cm) long bearing small yellowish green unisexual flowers of both sexes **Fruit:** ovoid, 2 in. (5 cm) long, deep orange to deep red when ripe, in large pendent masses **Growth rate:** moderate as a seedling, rather fast thereafter **Climate:** 10b and 11, marginal in warm parts of 10a **Exposure:** part shade when young, sun when older **Soil:** deep, sandy, slightly acidic, humus laden **Water needs:** moderate to high; often survives drought conditions but usually looks terrible **Salt tolerance:** none **Indoors:** only with intense light and good air circulation **Seed germination:** easy but sporadic; within three to six months if fresh and sown in warmth and moisture

Foxtail palm is similar to royal palm (*Roystonea regia*) but not as massive. It is among the best species for creating the "royal look" when planted in lines along an avenue or other promenades and as a canopy-scape is nearly unrivaled. Beware of

*Wodyetia bifurcata*, fruit, in Florida.

*Wodyetia bifurcata*, in Australia. Paul Craft

planting it too deeply in the ground, a practice which usually results in slow death for the plant.

## Zombia antillarum
### Zombi palm

**Distribution:** semiarid plains and hills on Hispaniola **Growth habit:** densely clustering **Height & width:** 10–15 ft. (3–4.5 m) tall, 12 ft. (4 m) wide **Trunk(s):** wrapped in a fantastic reticulate network of light to dark brown fibers, many parts of which are 4- to 6-in. (10- to 15-cm) long needle-like projections **Crownshaft:** none **Leaves:** palmate, semicircular, 3 ft. (90 cm) wide, divided into lance-shaped segments that extend halfway to two thirds into the blade, dull to dark lustrous green above, decidedly gray, grayish green, or even bluish gray beneath **Flower clusters:** spikes 18 in. (45 cm) long with a few yellowish branches bearing white bisexual flowers **Fruit:** round, ½–¾ in. (12–18 mm) wide, white when ripe **Growth rate:** slow **Climate:** 10 and 11, marginal in warmest parts of 9b **Exposure:** part sun to full sun **Soil:** any well-drained medium including an alkaline one **Water needs:** low, but grows slightly faster and looks better with regular irrigation **Salt tolerance:** medium **Indoors:** not very good **Seed germination:** easy; within three months if fresh

This palm is exceptionally beautiful in a site where its almost unique stems can be seen. Since its spininess is confined to the stems themselves, it can be used in intimate or close-up situations. Its natural tendency is to form dense clumps that obscure the trunks, resulting in a large mound of foliage in which not only the trunks but also the shape of the leaves is obscured. Thus, some judicious pruning out of the stems reveals not only the wondrous woven fibers and their spiny projections but also the ghostly white fruits in season.

*Zombia antillarum.* Paul Craft

*Zombia antillarum*, spiny stem, in Florida.

# USDA HARDINESS ZONE MAP

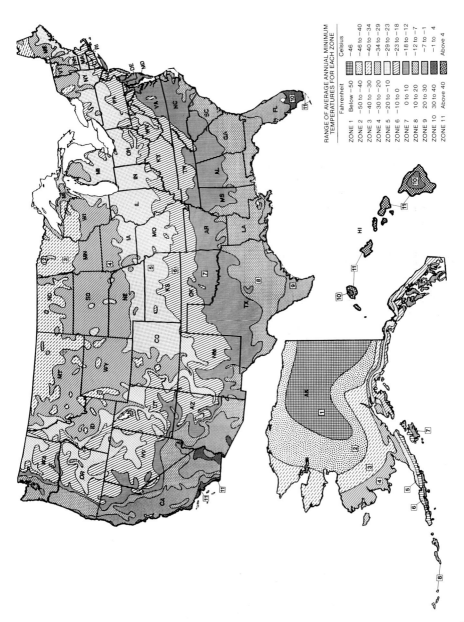

**RANGE OF AVERAGE ANNUAL MINIMUM TEMPERATURES FOR EACH ZONE**

| | Fahrenheit | Celsius |
|---|---|---|
| ZONE 1 | Below −50 | −46 |
| ZONE 2 | −50 to −40 | −46 to −40 |
| ZONE 3 | −40 to −30 | −40 to −34 |
| ZONE 4 | −30 to −20 | −34 to −29 |
| ZONE 5 | −20 to −10 | −29 to −23 |
| ZONE 6 | −10 to 0 | −23 to −18 |
| ZONE 7 | 0 to 10 | −18 to −12 |
| ZONE 8 | 10 to 20 | −12 to −7 |
| ZONE 9 | 20 to 30 | −7 to −1 |
| ZONE 10 | 30 to 40 | −1 to 4 |
| ZONE 11 | Above 40 | Above 4 |

# EUROPEAN HARDINESS ZONE MAP

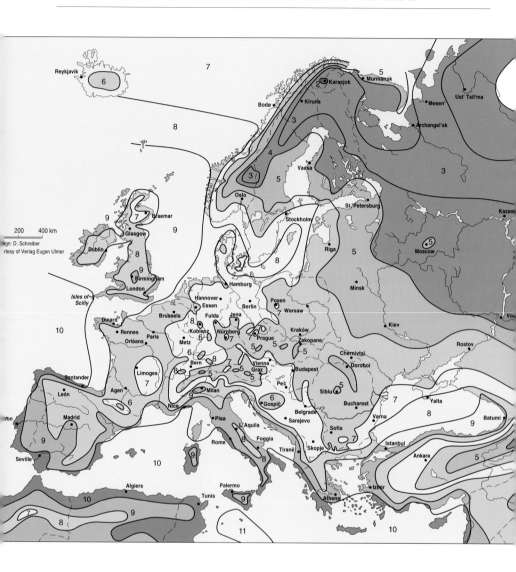

# NURSERY SOURCES

## United Kingdom

Amulree Exotics
Norwich Road
Fundenhall
Norfolk NR16 1EL
44 (01508) 488101
http://www.turn-it-tropical.co.uk

Chiltern Seeds
Bortree Stile, Ulverston
Cumbria, LA12 7PB
44 (01229) 581137
http://www.chilternseeds.co.uk

Hyde Cottage Palms and Exotics
Church Road
Crowle
Worcestershire WR7 4AT
44 (01905) 381632
http://www.palmsandexotics.co.uk

Mulu Nurseries
Longdon Hill
Wickhamford, Evesham
Worcestershire WR11 7RP
44 (01386) 833171
http://www.mulu.co.uk

The Palm Centre
Ham Central Nursery
Ham Street, Ham
Richmond, Surrey TW10 7HA
44 (02082) 556191
http://www.thepalmcentre.co.uk

The Palm Farm
Thornton Curtis
North Lincolnshire DN39 6XF
44 (01469) 531232
http://www.thepalmfarm.com

The Palm House
8 North Street
Ottery St. Mary
Devon EX11 1DR
44 (01404) 815450
http://www.thepalmhouse.co.uk

## United States

Aloha Tropicals
P.O. Box 6042
Oceanside, California 92054
(760) 631-2880
http://www.alohatropicals.com

Floribunda Palms and Exotics
P.O. Box 635
Mountain View, Hawaii 96771
(866) 966-8003
http://www.floribundapalms.com

Golden Gate Palm Nursery
P.O. Box 1172
Lafayette, California 94549
(925) 325-PALM
http://www.goldengatepalms.com

Good Earth Nursery
I-15 & Mission Road
Fallbrook, California 92028
(800) 662-5177
http://www.palms4u.com

J. D. Andersen Nursery
2790 Marvinga Lane
Fallbrook, California 92028
(760) 723-2907
http://www.jdandersen.com

Jungle Music Palms and Cycads
3233 Brant Street
San Diego, California 92103
(619) 291-4605
http://www.junglemusic.net

Kapoho Palm
P.O. Box 3
Pahoa, Hawaii 96778
(808) 936-2580
http://www.growpalms.com

Nickel Palm Nursery
29343 Merced Avenue
Shafter, California 93263
(661) 746-9999
http://www.nickelpalmnursery.com

Palm Island Nursery Outlet
3525 Stony Point Road
Santa Rosa, California 95407
(707) 585-8100
http://www.palmislandnursery.com

Parkway Nursery
5050 El Camino Real
Carlsbad, California 92008
(760) 438-2988
http://www.parkwaypalms.com

Plant Delights Nursery
9241 Sauls Road
Raleigh, North Carolina 27603
(919) 772-4794
http://www.plantdelights.com

Stokes Tropicals
4806 East Old Spanish Trail
Jeanerette, Louisiana 70544
(337) 365-6998
http://www.stokestropicals.com

Yucca Do Nursery
P.O. Box 907
Hempstead, Texas 77445
(979) 826-4580
http://www.yuccado.com

# GLOSSARY

**bipinnate** a pinnate leaf whose primary leaflets have been replaced by separate and smaller stalks that then bear their leaflets with or without individual stalks.

**bract** a leaflike structure below a flower or an inflorescence. Palm inflorescences usually have several to many bracts.

**canopy-scape** a term used in this volume to describe the use of a palm in the landscape wherein the palm's crown floats above adjacent or lower vegetation.

**crownshaft** a term used only with pinnate-leaved palm species to denote a tubular or cylindrical shaft above the woody part of the trunk. The tube is more or less columnar and consists of the expanded and tightly packed leaf bases of the leaves presently on the palm.

**cultivar** a variety or form of a species that originates in cultivation and is not found naturally.

**endemic** confined to a particular region.

**genus, genera** a collection of plants bearing similar characters. The category in scientific classification that ranks below family and above species.

**glaucous** covered with a whitish or bluish bloom or a waxy or powdery substance that is easily rubbed away.

**leaf base** the lowest or bottom part of a leaf. A widened (often greatly so) portion of the bottom of the leaf's stalk.

**leaflet** the individual segment of a pinnate leaf.

**midrib** the main vein(s) of a leaf or, as used in this volume, the central stalk of a pinnate leaf.

**palmate** fanlike. A compound leaf with leaflets growing from a common point.

**pinnate** featherlike. A leaf with more than three leaflets growing from the central axis or midrib. The leaflets may grow on opposite sides of the midrib in a single flat plane or they may grow at angles to create a plumose effect.

**plumose** featherlike with the segments arising from the midrib in more than one plane and resulting in a boalike appearance.

**species** the fundamental unit of biological classification, representing a group of closely related individual plants or animals.

**spine** a sharp protrusion on a leaf, branch, or stem. Used in this volume in its broad, nontechnical sense.

**stilt roots** large, aerial roots at or near the base of a palm's trunk or stem, which usually provide support and stability to the tree and which are usually in the form of a cone. Also called prop roots.

# FURTHER READING

Blombery, Alec, and Tony Rodd. 1989. *Palms of the World: Their Cultivation, Care, and Landscape Use*. London: Angus and Robertson.

Boyer, Keith. 1992. *Palms and Cycads Beyond the Tropics*. Queensland, Australia: Palm and Cycad Societies of Australia.

Broschat, Timothy K., and Alan W. Meerow. 2000. *Ornamental Palm Horticulture*. Gainesville, Florida: University Press of Florida.

Dransfield, John, and Henk Beentje. 1995. *The Palms of Madagascar*. London: Board of Trustees of the Royal Botanic Gardens, Kew.

Ellison, Don, and Anthony Ellison. 2001. *Betrock's Cultivated Palms of the World*. Hollywood, Florida: Betrock Information Systems.

Gibbons, Martin. 1993. *Palms*. Secaucus, New Jersey: Chartwell Books.

Henderson, Andrew, Gloria Galeano, and Rodrigo Bernal. 1995. *Palms of the Americas*. Princeton, New Jersey: Princeton University Press.

Hodel, Donald R. 1992. *Chamaedorea Palms*. Lawrence, Kansas: The International Palm Society.

Hodel, Donald R., ed. 1998. *The Palms and Cycads of Thailand*. Lawrence, Kansas: Allen Press.

Hodel, Donald R., and Jean-Christophe Pintaud. 1998. *The Palms of New Caledonia*. Lawrence, Kansas: Allen Press.

Jones, David L. 1995. *Palms Throughout the World*. Washington, D.C.: Smithsonian Institution Press.

Riffle, Robert Lee, and Paul Craft. 2003. *An Encyclopedia of Cultivated Palms*. Portland, Oregon: Timber Press.

Stewart, Lynette. 1994. *Palms and Cycads of the World*. Sydney, Australia: Angus and Robertson.

# INDEX

233